THE PUBLIC EXPENDITURE PROCESS
LEARNING BY DOING

Edited by **David Heald** and **Richard Rose**

Based on proceedings of a
Public Finance Foundation
seminar at Nuneham Park,
November 1986, sponsored by
Price Waterhouse.

Public Finance Foundation   *with*   **Price Waterhouse**
3, Robert Street,   1 London Bridge,
London WC2N 6BH   London SE1 9QL

Received :

Location :

Production: Inprint of Luton Ltd./T.A.F. Design Associates

Contents

		Page
Preface	Ian Beesley	(vii)
1. Introduction	Edmund Dell	1

Part I

2. Simulating decisions on public expenditure	Francis Terry	5
Annex A: Participants in the Simulation		12
Annex B: Assessor's guidelines		13
Annex C: Notes on the use of this volume as a teaching aid		16
3. Results of simulation: a Treasury view	Michael Posner and David Heald	19
4. Learning from experience	Richard Rose and Phillip Davies	37
5. Reflections of spending ministers		
Defence:	David Greenwood	51
Foreign & Commonwealth Office:	William Wallace	53
Agriculture, Fisheries & Food:	Allan Buckwell	54
Energy:	Graham Hadley	55
Employment:	Mark Cornelius	56
Transport:	Stephen Glaister	57
Environment:	George Jones	60
Home Office & Lord Chancellor's Department:	Nicholas Deakin	61
Health & Social Security:	Michael O'Higgins	62
Scotland:	James Ross	64
6. Postcripts	Ian Beesley	67
	George Jones	69
	Andrew Likierman	70

Part II

7. The Bid Book: Introduction and Summary Tables   73
7.1   Defence   82
       7.2   Foreign & Commonwealth Office   87
       7.3   Agriculture, Fisheries & Food   91
       7.4   Trade & Industry   94
       7.5   Energy   98
       7.6   Employment   103
       7.7   Transport   111
       7.8   Environment   120
       7.9   Home Office   130
       7.10 Education & Science   138
       7.11 Health & Social Security   139
       7.12 Scotland   146

       Citations   153

Attendance at weekend seminar at Nuneham Park, 7-9 November 1986

Participants:

Mr Ian Beesley	Price Waterhouse
Dr Daniel Beeton	Public Finance Foundation
Professor Allan Buckwell	Wye College, University of London
Mr Mark Cornelius	Employment Institute
Dr Phillip Davies	University of Strathclyde
Professor Nicholas Deakin	University of Birmingham
Rt. Hon. Edmund Dell	Public Finance Foundation
Professor Stephen Glaister	London School of Economics
Dr David Greenwood	University of Aberdeen
Mr Graham Hadley	Central Electricity Generating Board
Mr David Heald	University of Glasgow
Miss Sarah Hegarty	*Public Finance & Accountancy*
Sir Douglas Henley	former Comptroller & Auditor General
Mr Noel Hepworth	Public Finance Foundation
Mr Geoffrey Hulme	Public Finance Foundation
Mr Daniel Jeffreys	Cazenove & Co
Professor George Jones	London School of Economics
Mr Malcolm Levitt	Public Finance Foundation
Mr Andrew Likierman	London Business School
Mr Martin Lyne	Price Waterhouse
Mr Michael O'Higgins	University of Bath
Mr Michael Posner	European Science Foundation
Professor Richard Rose	University of Strathclyde
Mr James Ross	University of Strathclyde
Ms Judith Sutcliffe	Public Finance Foundation
Mr Francis Terry	Public Finance Foundation
Mr Tony Travers	North East London Polytechnic
Dr William Wallace	Royal Institute of International Affairs
Mr Tom Walls	Price Waterhouse

Preface

It was a real pleasure for Price Waterhouse to sponsor the seminar which simulated Cabinet discussion of public expenditure programmes.

This event promised a practical insight into how collective decisions at Cabinet and in the Star Chamber might operate. Of course, the assumptions, conventions and actual circumstances of a public expenditure round could not be replicated in full. But, as the material in this book shows, there were some surprises in how 'ministers' found themselves behaving. Participants came away, perhaps, with more sympathy for the dilemmas which their real-life counterparts face. There were lessons too, as the individual contributions here bring out.

Though theory is always important, there can never be a substitute for practice. Price Waterhouse are committed to providing clients with practical recommendations which will bring improved results. That commitment covers public sector issues and we are proud to join with the Public Finance Foundation and the participants in describing what happened one weekend in Oxfordshire when we were the Cabinet.

Ian Beesley, Price Waterhouse

1. Introduction

Edmund Dell

This book describes a simulation of Cabinet government at work. The subject matter of our simulation was the control of public expenditure.

There is much discussion about the substance of public expenditure and whether its share in GDP is too high or too low, and whether it is as well administered as it might be. There is some discussion as to the best methods of deciding relative priorities within public expenditure. There is relatively little discussion about the processes through which the major political decisions are actually made. Major government decisions in this country are supposed to be collectively taken. Once taken, all ministers are supposed to be bound to them by a system of collective responsibility. This country's governmental traditions dictate that collective decision-making is, for our kind of government, the optimal method, and collective responsibility the appropriate cement. Yet the actual procedures by which such decisions are made are little studied.

The Public Finance Foundation has taken these procedures as a suitable subject for study. In 1985 and again in 1986 we organised weekend seminars on the subject. Both these seminars attracted a very high and experienced quality of participation. Though conducted under a modified version of 'Chatham House' rules, informative reports have been published (Public Finance Foundation 1985, 1986). Yet discussion even with the most experienced participants can take the subject only so far. Experience of collective decision-taking in government is difficult to transfer and yet is essential to understanding. As it was unlikely that we would be admitted to 10 Downing Street to observe, let alone participate in, the Cabinet at work, we decided on a rather ambitious experiment. We would simulate the Cabinet at work. We would see whether the simulation could be made sufficiently lifelike to yield useful lessons.

We started with three framework assumptions. The first was that in any one year it is necessary to have some ceiling on the quantity of public expenditure. The second was that the total of departmental claims, when initially presented, would exceed that ceiling by a substantial margin. The third was that decisions about quantities and priorities nevertheless have to be taken. These assumptions were in themselves uncontroversial. But in our simulation, as in real life government, they led on to fierce controversy.

Some colleagues in the simulation lamented the lack of a political manifesto. I think they overestimate the philosophical cohesion within British governments. I think also they underestimate the speed with which departmental concerns overcome manifesto commitments, whatever the ideology. In this connection therefore I had a private fourth assumption: faced by the problems of controlling public expenditure, any group of knowledgeable and intelligent people would behave in essentially the same way, whatever their political predilections.

In real life, the responsibility for reconciling the disparity between the ceiling and the departmental claims lies in the hands of a group of ministers with different ideologies (even though normally of the same party), ministers with competing priorities, varying powers of persuasion, unequal status within their party, and competitive ambitions. That being so, it was perfectly acceptable for our purposes to gather our team together on the basis of their expertise rather than of their politics. Only private knowledge would have enabled me to identify the political allegiance of the members of this 'Cabinet'. In respect of most of them, I do not know to this day. But I found the conduct of all of them, charged as they were with notional responsibility for government departments in the affairs of which they were expert, remarkably reminiscent of an actual Cabinet at work.

Many would argue, and some did, that we lacked the resources to simulate with anything like accuracy the actual workings of a Cabinet in travail over public expenditure. In an important respect this criticism is justified. We had neither the time nor the money. Above all we did not have the civil service. I do not think that that is the end of the matter. The processes of collective decision-making in government are important and unfamiliar. To give a small group of high-powered people a taste of the process of negotiation and fudging that lies behind public expenditure White Papers is, in my view, a valuable educational exercise even if our simulation could not possibly replicate real life. Nor can it be neglected that the processes by which decisions are taken themselves influence the outcome. The outcome can only be understood if the processes are better understood. I do not apologise for encouraging an attempt to make them better understood, imperfect though that attempt must be. The simulation suggested many questions. Not the least important is whether the process is consistent with an optimal, or even a good, outcome.

2

I chaired the whole proceedings except those of the 'Star Chamber'. As the only participant of the enterprise who had served in a Cabinet, I tried to provide the right atmosphere by being rather sharp with colleagues who, in my opinion, were making bad points, but attentive to those who really had a case to argue and were arguing it well. On the other hand, I did not attempt to impose 'my' solution. Rather, I wanted my colleagues to come to a collective agreement if they could and then consider whether it was really a good outcome, let alone the best. What they thought about the method of coming to that collective agreement, I must leave them to say in the course of the comments that they make elsewhere in this book. My own comment would be that the desire to agree at all overcame any impulse to force any colleague into a corner. This was assisted by the Chancellor's initial generosity (not greater than that of the actual Chancellor of the Exchequer) and by the device of a further input of £3bn from unspecified privatisation. As a result, my colleagues were able to come to a collective agreement without any resignations being threatened let alone implemented. One lesson for any future simulation would be to make the exercise much tougher by defining a crisis scenario.

I must emphasis that the Public Finance Foundation is not to be identified with any particular attitude to the level of public expenditure or with the views of the particular ministers involved in this exercise. They were all very good. Their knowledge was impressive. Their idiosyncracies were manageable. But the Public Finance Foundation denies any responsibility for any of them.

This simulation was made possible by the generosity of Price Waterhouse in sponsoring it, and by the ready willingness of our 'Cabinet' of experts. On their shoulders it fell to undertake the necessary preliminary work in preparing the Bid Book on which the exercise was based. They were then ready to sacrifice a weekend to the actual proceedings. I am grateful to them all. I hope they enjoyed it.

2.   Simulating Decisions on Public Expenditure

Francis Terry

Background

The scientific study of decision-making has a substantial pedigree, dating back to the pioneer work of American social scientists in the 1930s. Indeed, the intellectual problems it confronts, and the concepts it deploys, have their origins much further back than that, in the literature of philosophy and mathematics.   Present day research on decision-making now accounts for 192 separate project entries in *Current Research in Britain in 1986* (British Library 1986), with much other work being unrecorded there. The subject is recognised as having practical applications in such fields as defence planning, business policy and management; but it is not (as yet) widely understood or applied in public service organisations.   One reason may be that, to many public service policy-makers and managers, the political background against which they work appears incompatible with the 'rational self-interest' approach of the commercial firm.   There are, however, techniques (Mack 1971) for taking into account unpredictable or non-rational factors in decision analysis, and perhaps these deserve to be better known in public service industries and authorities.

The seminar referred to in this book was conducted in a spirit of academic enquiry, but it was not intended as a controlled scientific experiment, nor was it concerned to prove or disprove any particular theory.   It began as an attempt to rehearse the arguments commonly advocated for public spending programmes of various kinds, and to illuminate the problem of reconciling, within a fixed total, the competing financial claims of these programmes.

The idea of a seminar which would simulate aspects of the decision-making process on public expenditure grew out of two previous events organised by the Public Finance Foundation and chaired by the Rt. Hon. Edmund Dell. The first of these, held in July 1985 at Nuneham Park in Oxfordshire, brought together academics and financial managers, with representatives of local government, trades unions and City institutions to consider the machinery of collective decision-making in government. The seminar included presentations on national planning in France, and two American viewpoints on public expenditure control; sponsorship was provided by Deloitte, Haskins & Sells. A report of the proceedings, conducted under 'Chatham House' rules, was subsequently published as *Collective Decision-Making in Government* (Public Finance Foundation 1985).

The sequel to the Nuneham Park seminar was at Eynsham Hall, Oxfordshire, in January 1986, and focused more specifically on public expenditure decision-making. Participants this time included serving civil servants from HM Treasury and spending departments; sponsorship was afforded by Henderson Pension Fund Management Ltd. The proceedings, again under 'Chatham House' rules, were reported in *Collective Decision-Making on Public Expenditure* (Public Finance Foundation 1986). In the course of the seminars, various key characteristics of the Public Expenditure Survey (PESC) system were isolated and discussed. Some of these related to the way in which public expenditure programmes are built up by departments, some to the quality of dialogue between the Treasury and departments and others to the method by which competing bids are reconciled at official and ministerial level. The roles of select committees, the Star Chamber and of a possible central policy review unit featured quite prominently in the discussions.

Objectives of this simulation

There was a feeling among some participants in the seminars that it would be an interesting exercise to try and simulate aspects of the public expenditure decision process; this was done at a third seminar which Price Waterhouse agreed to sponsor in November 1986. Such a novel exercise required careful preparation, and two exploratory meetings were held, on 11 April and 14 July 1986, with a variety of experts in particular fields of public policy. The first of these meetings was devoted to a discussion of feasibility, based on a proposal drawn up by Professor Richard Rose. Although one or two sceptical notes were sounded about the value of the outcome, there were no serious objections. The second meeting, held after the programme bids had been prepared, concentrated on the arrangements for the weekend seminar. By this time, the enthusiasm of the participants had built up to the point where it proved difficult to avoid some exchange of arguments likely to be used in the simulation itself!

The purpose of the seminar was to provide a means of exploring, through group discussions and negotiations, the problems of increasing or decreasing public expenditure by British central government today. The advantage of simulation is that it enables a variety of trial-and-error decision-making processes to be run through and evaluated; but what simulation seeks to avoid in terms of real-life risks, it may also lose in terms of verisimilitude. Nevertheless, there was widespread agreement among those consulted, including the sponsors, that the seminar could illustrate some important features of the public expenditure process, and this could be beneficial both in an educational sense and in identifying topics for further research and debate.

Ground rules

Discussions about public spending programmes in real life, and the resources available, are easily confused by arguments over whether a particular government in office has got its economic policy right, and correspondingly whether public spending needs to be constrained at a certain level. There is also an ever-present temptation among elected councillors and MPs (or their political opponents) to use special pleading in support of some particular needy case - though without necessarily offering realistic suggestions about where the extra resources are to be found. Part of the object of the seminar was to show how such temptations can, and indeed must, be faced up to in the real world of expenditure planning.

The ground rules of the seminar therefore required that there should be no right of challenge to the macroeconomic judgements of the simulation 'Chancellor of the Exchequer'. For plausible but unspecified reasons, total public spending over the next three years was to be held at certain target levels, and these levels could only be raised after all other possibilities for meeting the demands of spending programmes had been thoroughly examined. In any case, to do otherwise would destroy the point of the exercise. It was recognised, however, that the Contingency Reserve is an established instrument of public expenditure planning and, provided its use is strictly limited, it can play a part in reaching final agreement on programme totals.

Preliminary discussions soon showed that it would be too complex an undertaking to simulate the interplay between officials and ministers, and one 'spokesman' was therefore appointed for each main programme, whose role in the early stages of the exercise could be compared to that of a member of the Public Expenditure Survey Committee (after which the PESC system takes its name). Later, at the weekend seminar, they evolved into 'ministers' and are listed at Annex A to this chapter. They were expected to have a thorough working knowledge of the field they would represent, and a basic understanding of the PESC system. A number of them were either academics who had held a policy adviser post at some time, or vice versa. It was of paramount importance that the seminar should not be regarded by outside commentators, especially the press, as an exercise in replanning public expenditure from any particular political viewpoint. Spokesmen were therefore chosen who currently had no recognisable political life at national level.

In reality, changes from year to year in the distribution of resources between programmes can occur only at the margin. This is because a high proportion of spending in any given year is represented by existing commitments, and major shifts are possible only where institutions and manpower can be rapidly created or adapted to additional tasks - something it is seldom easy to do. Such a major practical constraint, which applies to all governments including those newly elected to office, had to be taken into account in the simulation exercise. A complete recasting of public expenditure was therefore ruled out, and the discussion started from the actual programme figures published in the 1986 public expenditure White Paper (Cmnd 9702, Treasury 1986a). Nevertheless, some significant changes in patterns of spending over a three-year period were proposed and part of the seminar debate indeed centred on how far some of these would be feasible in practice.

Spokesmen took full responsibility for programme costings, although the Co-ordinator, Professor Richard Rose, and the Assessor, David Heald, were available to give advice as necessary. There was one final constraint on spokesmen: in the event of an irreconcilable disagreement with colleagues, a threat of 'resignation' or request for 'transfer to other duties' would not be accepted!

Method

Each programme spokesman was required to brief himself on the essential points of the existing programme of government spending in the field for which he was to be responsible. This entailed careful study of the 1986 public expenditure White Paper and any other published documents likely to be relevant. The Assessor's guidelines were then circulated explaining that the government had decided to make £5bn of additional resources available in each of the three financial years 1987/88, 1988/89 and 1989/90; and these increases were to be divided among spending programmes in response to bids from departments. (The Assessor's guidelines are reproduced as Annex B to this chapter.) There was also a suggestion that economic or political circumstances might dictate a reduction in expenditure levels as against published plans, and that cuts would then have to be absorbed in selected programmes, as part of a follow-on exercise.

Taking the public expenditure White Paper figures for 1986/87 as a base line, each spokesman had to prepare a short reasoned case for his proposed programme of spending over the years 1987/88, 1988/89 and 1989/90; to prepare himself against a possible challenge to cut the existing published programme in Cmnd 9702; and to arm himself with points that could be used in the debate on other people's bids.

The statements of case were submitted to the Co-ordinator, Professor Richard Rose, for collation into a 'Bid Book'. This formed the basic working document for the seminar, and was circulated to all participants shortly before the simulation took place over the weekend of 7-9 November 1986. The Bid Book is reproduced in full as Chapter 7, both because of its intrinsic interest and so that teachers and students in public administration can use it to repeat the exercise in collective decision-making for themselves. Additional notes about using the material in this way are at Annex C to this chapter.

Two points need to be borne in mind when looking at the Bid Book entries for Education & Science and Trade & Industry. First, Professor Alan Little of Goldsmiths' College, University of London, was to have prepared the Education & Science bid. However, he asked to be relieved of any further involvement on health grounds and participants at the seminar were saddened to hear of his death. The Bid Book figures for Education & Science simply attributed to it increases for each year equal to the average percentage for the bids which had been received. This brief at the weekend seminar was taken at short notice by Andrew

Likierman of the London Business School who had previously been involved in the planning of the event, without having a spending portfolio. However, there was no discussion of the Education & Science figures. Second, Mr. Daniel Jeffreys had agreed to take on the Trade & Industry portfolio while working at the Confederation of British Industry, but the period of preparation for the seminar coincided with a job move. Although he played his part in the seminar, he has been unable to provide the written text supporting his programme numbers, or to provide subsequent reflections on the seminar.

It came as no surprise to find that the bids from departmental spokesmen considerably exceeded the programme totals published in Cmnd 9702 - by over £23bn in 1987/88, for example (see Table 7A of the Bid Book). But spending decisions involve differences of opinion about increases, at other times about savings, and often a combination of increases and cuts. A consolidated list of proposed spending changes is at Table 7B of the Bid Book. In some cases the net increases in cash sought by some departments were relatively minor; indeed the Energy programme was seen as making a net contribution to the Exchequer over the plan period.

The programme for the seminar was left quite flexible, so that there would be scope for negotiation both in full session, and privately on the sidelines. The proceedings were observed by a number of experts who did not hold a brief for any individual programme nor take part in the negotiations. Their role was to comment at intervals on the debate, to raise additional questions and generally to appraise the realism of the exercise. From these 'stock-taking' intervals, some issues for further detailed discussion emerged, and these were examined in the closing session of the seminar. They are written up in Chapter 6 by the people who initially raised them.

The seminar opened with a short explanation by the spokesman in the role of 'Chancellor of the Exchequer' (Michael Posner) of the hypothetical economic and financial background against which overall spending totals had been set. Each departmental spokesman in turn put his case and faced questioning on it. This part of the proceedings could be compared to the closing stages of the 'bilateral' discussions that take place each summer between officials in Whitehall and later between departmental ministers and the Chief Secretary to the Treasury. Great skill is of course required, in the real world, to handle such 'bilaterals' effectively: a minister's performance can make or break his reputation with the public services, industries or agencies for which he is responsible; it can help to reinforce (or alternatively may undermine) a minister's credibility with his officials; and it may have much wider implications for his standing among political colleagues, in the House of Commons, and in the media. One key test of tactical ability is to know when to compromise on a bid, and when to hold out in the hope that an appeal to higher authority - ultimately the full Cabinet - will succeed.

Recent years have seen the development of the Star Chamber as a mechanism for arbitrating on departmental bids that have failed to be reconciled in previous discussions. At the weekend seminar held as part of the current exercise, it initially proved impossible for the programmes to be reduced by sufficient amounts to fit within the prescribed spending totals. Reduced programme figures proposed by the Chancellor were unacceptable to the ministers. A Star Chamber was therefore constituted of five participants to interview separately the recalcitrant ministers in detail, and to reach a verdict on their cases. Following these deliberations, the Chancellor determined the final allocation of resources to each of the twelve spending programmes. In a short presentation, the basis of the allocation, and hence the solution to the exercise, was justified to the full seminar.

The outcome figures for the exercise are reproduced in Table 3.3 and are discussed in three chapters: Chapter 3 by Michael Posner and David Heald which records the results and comments from a Treasury viewpoint; Chapter 4 by Richard Rose and Phillip Davies on the wider implications of the simulation; and Chapter 5 in which each spending minister reflects upon how well he had presented his case, and the lessons to be learned.

Annex A: Participants in the Simulation

Prime Minister	Edmund Dell
Chancellor of the Exchequer	Michael Posner
Foreign Secretary	William Wallace
Home Secretary	Nicholas Deakin
Secretary of State for Energy	Graham Hadley
Secretary of State for Defence	David Greenwood
Secretary of State for Agriculture, Fisheries & Food	Allan Buckwell
Secretary of State for Health & Social Security	Michael O'Higgins
Secretary of State for Scotland	James Ross
Secretary of State for Trade & Industry	Daniel Jeffreys
Secretary of State for Environment	George Jones
Secretary of State for Transport	Stephen Glaister
Chief Secretary	David Heald
Secretary of State for Employment	Mark Cornelius
Secretary of State for Education & Science	Andrew Likierman
Cabinet Secretary	Richard Rose

Annex B: Assessor's Guidelines

1. The Chancellor's judgement is that the nation will be able to afford an increase in public expenditure over the existing plans contained in the 1986 White Paper (Cmnd 9702). Consequently, £5bn will be added to those plans for each of the years 1987/88, 1988/89, 1989/90. In cash, the revised plan for 1987/88 will be £148.9bn; this is £9.8bn up on 1986/87, an increase of 7.0%. This figure can be set against the 3.75% forecast increase in the GDP deflator. Equivalent figures for the later years are as follows. At £153.7bn, 1988/89 plan is £4.8bn up in cash over 1987/88 (3.2% compared to forecast increase in GDP deflator of 3.5%). At £158.2bn, 1989/90 is £4.8bn up in cash over 1988/89 (2.9% compared with 3.0%). It should be stressed that these cash increases must cover all forms of change, inflation as well as policy.

2. All these figures can be read off the appropriate lines of Table 2.1: for example, revised planning total (line 11); year-on-year cash increases (line 12 for absolute amount and line 13 for percentage); and forecast GDP deflators (line 7). Throughout this exercise, the starting point is Cmnd 9702.

3. Departments should send to Francis Terry, at Public Finance Foundation, 3 Robert Street, London WC2N 6BH, on or before 14th June 1986, estimates of outturn for 1986/87, and plans for 1987/88, 1988/89 and 1989/90. Two tables are required; exemplifications for Health and Personal Social Services are attached:

    (i)   Table A is a main programme table for 1987/88, showing for each line:

        (a)   1986/87 expenditure (from Cmnd 9702);
        (b)   revised expenditure plan for 1987/88;
        (c)   absolute year-on-year increase over 1986/87; and
        (d)   percentage year-on-year increase over 1986/87.

(ii)   Table B is a main programme table giving revised expenditure plans for 1987/88 and 1988/89 and plans for 1989/90, showing for each line:

(a)   1986/87 plan (from Cmnd 9702);
(b)   estimated outturn for 1986/87;
(c)   revised 1987/88 plan;
(d)   revised 1988/89 plan;
(e)   1989/90 plan (the new horizon year);
(f)   absolute change, 1989/90 plan over 1986/87 plan; and
(g)   percentage change, 1989/90 plan over 1986/87 plan.

The general presumption is that the appropriate level of detail is the sub-programmes in the Cmnd 9702 chapters (which are distributed with this letter). Defence is an obvious exception, where the submission should relate to the main heads in the Defence Budget rather than just the summary data in Cmnd 9702-II.

4.   Justifications of cash increases shown for 1987/88 over 1986/87 in Table A should distinguish wherever possible between:

(i)   changes in the cost of providing the current level of service because of an increase in the number or mix of clients;

(ii)   increases in public sector costs above the projected change in the GDP deflator (the Relative Price Effect);

(iii)   policy changes; and

(iv)   other estimating changes.

Furthermore, Departments should make clear in their submissions both the 'part-year' and 'full-year' cost of changes.

5.   The Assessor (David Heald) is available to give advice upon the interpretation of these guidelines and to explain any point of difficulty (tel: 041-339 8855 ext 4064/6305 or 041-946 6184).

Table 2.1: Public Expenditure Plans to 1989/90, £bn

	84/85	85/86	86/87	87/88	88/89	89/90
1. Programmes	131.7	137.0	139.7	142.3	145.4	
2. Central privatisation proceeds	-2.1	-2.6	-4.7	-4.7	-4.7	
3. Adjustments		-0.2	-0.4			
4. Contingency Reserve			4.5	6.3	8.0	
5. Planning Total (as Cmnd 9702)	129.6	134.2	139.1	143.9	148.7	
6. Year-on-year cash increase			4.9	4.8	4.8	
7. Year-on-year GDP deflator			3.75%	3.75%	3.50%	3.00%
8. Stand-still cash at GDP deflator			5.0	5.2	5.0	4.5
9. Chancellor's bonus				5.0	5.0	5.0
10. Shortfall		-0.3				
11. Revised Planning Total	129.6	133.9	139.1	148.9	153.7	158.2
12. Year-on-year cash increase (amount)		4.3	5.2	9.8	4.8	4.5
13. Year-on-year cash increase (%)		3.3%	3.9%	7.0%	3.2%	2.9%
14. Programmes	131.7	137.0	144.2	147.3	150.4	154.9
15. Central privatisation proceeds	-2.1	-2.6	-4.7	-4.7	-4.7	-4.7
16. Adjustments		-0.2	-0.4			
Contingency Reserve:						
17. - committed				0.2	0.2	0.2
18. - uncommitted				6.1	7.8	7.8
19. Shortfall		-0.3				
20. Planning Total	129.6	133.9	139.1	148.9	153.7	158.2
21. Additional sums for programmes over Cmnd 9702				5.0	5.0	5.0

Annex C: Notes on the Use of this Volume as a Teaching Aid

One of the reasons for documenting the simulation is that it provides a basis for others who are interested in the public expenditure process to try it out for themselves. The sponsors of the seminar, Price Waterhouse, were concerned that the educational value of the event should be fully exploited, and these notes are intended to help teachers and students of public administration and economics to make practical use of the material. It is, of course, not necessary to spend an entire weekend in discussion and reconciliation of public expenditure programme totals; on the other hand, the value of using this book is greatly enhanced if the exercise is properly prepared for and is supported by relevant background reading.

An essential source of reference, prior to attempting a simulation exercise, is *The Management of Public Spending* (Treasury, 1986d). This concise volume, published in May 1986 and available from the Treasury for £1.00 plus postage, explains in simple terms how public expenditure plans are annually reviewed and updated. It covers the key elements on which the simulation is based.

It is also recommended that participants in a simulation should examine the actual presentation of public expenditure programmes in the public expenditure White Papers. These are normally published by HMSO each January, in two volumes, the first dealing with the overall strategy for public spending in relation to economic and other objectives; and the second dealing with the detailed composition of individual programmes, as well as providing analysis of spending by central government, local authorities and public corporations. It is important that those who are allocated the role of spokespersons for spending departments should understand the kind of arguments that carry weight in the determination of public expenditure priorities. Moreover, in playing out the simulation, they may wish to introduce new policies and alterations in the composition of their programme if they think that this would strengthen their case. The simulation exercise thus provides a framework for understanding how Whitehall departments formulate and present their case for resources, as well as being an exercise in collective decision-making. There are, of course, many other references on public spending to which students can be referred. To give the flavour of how decisions are reached collectively by ministers, it may be helpful to refer to the reports of the two earlier seminars which stimulated the present exercise (Public Finance Foundation, 1985, 1986).

After studying the public expenditure process as it currently operates, and having examined the presentation of spending programmes, it is suggested that each student, or pair of students, could be allotted a programme and given a copy of the relevant chapter of the Bid Book. This will provide the student with an outline script on which a more exhaustive case for resources can be based. It may be more testing as an exercise if the student does not see the material relating to other programmes. It is also open to the tutor either to focus attention on the arguments supporting the figures in the Bid Book, or to allow variations in the proposed spending figures for each programme as well. This latter approach may have the effect of accentuating the discrepancy between the total of bids and the total which the Chancellor is prepared to concede. Another option for the tutor would be to concentrate attention on a particular year (as the simulation at Nuneham Park did) or on a sequence of years to illustrate how trends in expenditure have to be managed in relation to economic policy. But the main object of the exercise should be to demonstrate that any government in office has to resolve competing priorities and to contain spending within pre-set limits. Finally, it should be required reading for each student to understand the Assessor's guidelines, on the basis of which the bids were prepared.

Depending on the number of students taking part, the simulation should last between a half-day and a full-day. The tutor could take the role either of Prime Minister (or perhaps the more subdued role of Chairman), and a staff colleague could play the role of Chancellor. It will also be helpful to appoint a person who can keep track of spending figures as they are put forward and to check these against the limit set by the Chancellor. Alternatively, the tutor may wish to adopt the role of Assessor or of observer, and to appoint students to these central roles. Students should be encouraged to present their case as concisely as possible and to focus on arguments which they think would carry weight in an economic and political context. It may therefore be helpful if the tutor were to sketch the hypothetical political background against which the simulation is presumed to be taking place as a counterpart to the Chancellor's depiction of the economic context. The tutor could, for example, explain that the government has either just been elected with, say, a large majority and is thus confident about its future, or that it is approaching a general election after an unpopular period and anxious to appease public opinion. After the statement of case by each spokesperson, the simulation can be extended by constituting a Star Chamber to resolve particularly awkward conflicts of priorities. Alternatively, the tutor may simply arbitrate between programmes on the basis of the arguments presented.

At the conclusion, it will probably be helpful for students and the tutor to detach themselves from the roles which they have been playing and to discuss in a dispassionate way how effectively they felt each programme was presented, how well it fared in terms of securing resources, and perhaps whether the final outcome would be likely to command support in Parliament, the civil service and among the wider public. For comparison, reference can be made to the outcome of the Nuneham Park seminar.

3. Results of Simulation: A Treasury View

Michael Posner and David Heald

The simulation

The Assessor's guidelines

It is essential to understand the context within which the simulation was designed: particularly the Conservative Government's announced intention of holding public expenditure constant in real terms and thereby reducing the public expenditure/GDP ratio as GDP expands. The Assessor's guidelines are reproduced in full as Annex B to Chapter 2. The simulation was concerned with three years: 1987/88, 1988/89, 1989/90. The planning totals for the first two of these years, as set out in the 1986 public expenditure White Paper (Cmnd 9702, Treasury 1986a) were £143.9bn and £148.7bn respectively. The guidelines automatically granted extra money to the extent of the forecast GDP deflator (taken from Treasury 1986b) to produce a total which could be described as 'standstill cash', but which would still imply a squeeze on those programmes where costs rise faster than the GDP deflator. On top of this, the 'simulation' Chancellor of the Exchequer granted a flat bonus of £5bn in each of the three years. Because this bonus was not cumulative, it therefore was of much more significant benefit in the first planning year (1987/88). The new horizon year (1989/90) which came into the simulation exercise was calculated simply as the 1988/89 planning total revalued by the forecast GDP deflator, plus the £5bn bonus.

Much of the discussion would inevitably focus on the spending programmes within the planning total but it is important to note the assumptions which were made about the Contingency Reserve and central privatisation proceeds. The former represents part of the planning total which is not earmarked to programmes, with the objective of providing a buffer so that pressing spending claims can subsequently be met without prejudicing the planning total. Central privatisation proceeds denote the revenue from the sale of public sector assets which directly accrues to the Treasury. The much-criticised accounting presentation treats such proceeds as negative expenditure, thus reducing the declared planning total. The guidelines included quite high provisions for the Contingency Reserve, with the figures for the three planning years being set at £6.3bn, £8bn and £8bn (compared with the 1986 White Paper's provision of £4.5bn, £6.3bn and £8bn for its three planning years). In other words, the guidelines tried to hold the 1987/88 Contingency Reserve at the £6.3bn which had been fixed when 1987/88 was the second rather than the first of the years in the planning sequence. As for central privatisation proceeds, the cash available for programmes was higher than it would otherwise have been because of the assumption - still a matter for collective decision - that they would be sustained for a further year at the level of £4.7bn prevailing in the 1986 White Paper.

The guidelines were envisaged as a clear but cautious sign that the climate for public expenditure was changing. However, it was stressed that the extra resources being made available should be efficiently used: and that public expenditure policy should contribute, where appropriate, to the Government's aim of reduced unemployment. But, at the same time, departments were exhorted to pay particular attention to increasing efficiency through better management and by resource switching. Similarly, there was an emphasis upon continuing firm control of public sector costs. Departments were warned that the opportunity to expand services selectively would be lost if the rate of increase in public sector costs were to be significantly higher than the change in the GDP deflator (i.e. if there were to be a high Relative Price Effect).

The guidelines provided the framework for the submission of departmental bids and specified the format which was used consistently to produce departmental Table As (the first planning year 1987/88) and Table Bs (the final planning year 1989/90). A key table in the Bid Book is Table 7A which compares the simulation bids with the Treasury figures in the 1986 White Paper. The guidelines provided for a 1987/88 planning total of £148.9bn; the simulation bids came to £154.909bn, exceeding the guideline planning total by £6.009bn. The simulation bids for 1989/90 totalled £182.235bn which was £24,035bn above the guideline planning total of £158.2bn. If the guidelines were to be strictly followed, these italicised numbers were the amounts to be cut. But, at this stage of the exercise, there was a significant shift in the basis of the argument. A different calculation, made from Table 7A of the Bid Book, became the basis of the subsequent Cabinet discussions: this compared the 1989/90 bids with the 1986 White Paper figures for 1987/88, showing an increase of £38.335bn. A global allowance of £15bn was set against this apparent overbid of £38.335bn, thus giving the amount to be cut of £23.335bn. Although these two indicators of the amount to be cut in 1989/90, namely £24,035bn and £23,335bn, were of closely similar magnitudes, they were nevertheless composed of significantly different components as the Annex to this chapter makes clear. These differences did have some influence on the subsequent proceedings. This global allowance of £15bn had to cover the existing Cmnd 9702's £4.8bn to cover the transition from 1987/88 to 1988/90, and then both inflation from 1988/89 to 1989/90, as well as the new programme commitments being envisaged in the simulation.

The first Cabinet sessions

After the Prime Minister had set the scene for collective deliberations on public expenditure, the Chancellor reviewed the Bid Book figures. He stressed two particular years, 1987/88 and 1989/90, and announced that he wanted to focus attention upon the latter. Unless agreement could be reached to eliminate the excess bids for that year of £23.335bn, it would be impossible to reach sensible decisions on the earlier years. Reviewing the individual programmes, he ridiculed the size of the bids for Defence and Employment, but said that, while the Health & Social Security bid was unlikely to be accommodated within the planning total, he was impressed with the quality of that submission. He would not at this stage put a number on the reduction expected from that programme. The reductions which he asked for were described as giving a rough order of magnitude. They were not sufficient of themselves, as the reduction to the planning total would be only £17bn compared with an absolute minimum of £20bn. Those programmes not yet singled out were in no way spared the necessity of securing reductions against existing bids.

	£m
Defence	3,500
Employment	6,000
Transport	500
Home Office	1,000
Education & Science	1,000
Scotland	1,000
Other Departments	2,000
Reduction in Contingency Reserve	2,000
	17,000

Spending ministers then vigorously defended their programmes as in the Bid Book, stressing their own reasonableness: the Chancellor received some general support but no specific support in the form of volunteered reductions. The Foreign Secretary disassociated himself from the Defence bid. The Health & Social Security bid came under attack as excessive, particularly from the Secretary of State for Trade & Industry. The absence of any forward figures for central privatisation proceeds was sharply criticised by the Secretary of State for Education & Science who proposed a list of industrial candidates for privatisation, suggesting that £5bn a year could be found in this way. Support for privatisation came also from the Secretary of State for Trade & Industry who called for privatisation measures as a means of curbing the excessive demands of Health & Social Security and Education & Science. There was considerable criticism of the size of the Contingency Reserve.

The Secretary of State for the Environment argued forcefully that much of the expenditure under discussion was not actually under the control of the Cabinet, for example because it was spent by local authorities. When he proposed that the exercise should be recast, including only central grants to local authorities and not their expenditure, the Prime Minister ruled that decisions would this year have to be taken on the basis of the existing conventions but that Cabinet would be pleased to consider a paper proposing alternative rules for next year (see Chapter 6). Some ministers tried to broaden discussion towards a review of the Government's spending priorities, but the meeting was dominated by spending ministers directly under fire defending their programmes. The relationship between the expenditure in the Employment programme and in the Social Security programme quickly emerged as one of the most important technical issues, but one on which little reliable information seemed to be available. There are 'externalities' between the programmes: more spending on employment measures should, by reducing the number of unemployed, directly reduce the demand-led outlays of the Department of Health & Social Security. In terms of policy towards unemployment, it is in principle therefore necessary to look at both together.

The Prime Minister gave strong support to the Chancellor but no immediate progress was made towards securing expenditure reductions.

That evening, a brief meeting between the Prime Minister, the Chancellor and the Chief Secretary established the parameters for the rest of the weekend. It was decided to concentrate attention upon 1989/90, and to leave the first two years to be settled afterwards. The targets for cuts was trimmed back to £20bn and the principles enunciated which would form the basis of the alternative methods of achieving the cuts which would be put to Cabinet. The following day, the Chancellor put to Cabinet three possible alternatives as to how £20bn could be cut off the simulation bids in order to get back to a planning total of £162.235bn. In response to the previous Cabinet discussion, at which there had been support for using privatisation as a less painful means of curbing the planning total than actually cutting expenditure, privatisation proceeds of £3bn were reintroduced. However, reversing his offered reduction of £2bn, the Chancellor now insisted on increasing the Contingency Reserve by £1.5bn to £11.25bn because he simply did not believe that all the proposed cuts were politically acceptable (and considered that some ministers themselves knew that quite well). If clumsy and bad cuts are quickly cobbled together, there is a significant chance that at least some will never be implemented. Although other ministers derided this increase as simply a manoeuvre, there is an inverse relationship between the confidence which can be attached to expenditure reductions and the necessary size of the Contingency Reserve. Ministers worry most about the plans for programme expenditure, but, when the money is actually spent, the Contingency Reserve is released into programme expenditure.

At the previous day's Cabinet, spending ministers had frequently appealed to ideas of 'fairness', though often in ways which seemed to the Chancellor to embody arbitrary formulae. Following this, the second and third columns of Table 3.1 are constructed in the following ways. Option A interprets fairness in terms of equiproportional cuts on the 1989/90 bids, meaning that each programme gets 89.4% of its bid. (This holds except for Energy where the negative expenditure was subjected to a rough manual adjustment, rather than proportionalised.) Option B interprets the idea of fairness in terms of equiproportional increases on the 1986/87 base year, with each programme receiving in 1989/90 110.2% of that base level.

Having illustrated the effect of two alternative percentage adjustments, the Chancellor argued strongly that cuts against bids should be targeted selectively according to the Government's priorities. With the agreement

TABLE 3.1 SUMMARY OF THE CHANCELLOR'S ALTERNATIVES FOR 1989/90

£m

	Bids	Option A	Option B	Option C
Defence	22,375	20,005	20,420	19,875
Foreign & Commonwealth Office	2,204	1,971	2,159	1,970
Agriculture, Fisheries & Food	2,702	2,416	2,392	2,415
Trade & Industry	2,009	1,796	1,743	1,009
Energy	(300)	(500)	127	(500)
Employment	10,192	9,113	4,124	5,692
Transport	5,551	4,963	5,301	4,961
Environment	7,280	6,509	7,026	6,280
Home Office	6,476	5,790	6,097	5,788
Education & Science	17,424	15,579	15,784	16,424
Health & Social Security	71,964	64,342	66,861	67,964
Scotland	8,359	7,474	8,348	7,359
Other Departments	16,249	14,528	13,605	14,249
Total programmes	172,485	153,986	153,987	153,486
Contingency Reserve	9,750	11,250	11,250	11,750
Central privatisation proceeds		(3,000)	(3,000)	(3,000)
Planning total	182,235	162,236	162,237	162,236

Notes: A = equiproportional cuts on 1989/90 bid figures
B = equiproportional increases on 1986/87 base year
C = Chancellor's judgement at 23.00 hours on 7 November 1986

TABLE 3.2 THE EXPENDITURE DECISIONS UNDERLYING THE CHANCELLOR'S OPTION C FOR 1989/90

£m

Departments represented:

Employment	(4,500)
Health & Social Security	(4,000)
Defence	(2,500)
Environment	(1,000)
Scotland	(1,000)
Trade & Industry	(1,000)
Energy	(200)

Departments not represented:

Education & Science	(1,000)
Other Departments	(2,000)

leaving £1800m to be found from the four other departments (all of them represented ministerially in this simulation) on a proportional basis from 1989/90 bid, with a saving of £1800m being required out of an expenditure sub-total of £16,933. Thus:

Home Office	(688)
Transport	(590)
Agriculture, Fisheries & Food	(287)
Foreign & Commonwealth Office	(234)
Reduction in programmes	(18,999)
Central privatisation proceeds	(3,000)
Increase in Contingency Reserve	2,000
Reduction in planning total	(19,999)

of the Prime Minister, the Treasury had prepared Option C which reflected the Chancellor's judgements about the merits of the cases put up by spending ministers and, of course, the relative contribution which their departments make to both the planning total itself and to the total of excess bids. The specific expenditure decisions which underly Option C are shown in Table 3.2, thus proposing £19bn of expenditure cuts and a figure for central privatisation proceeds of £3bn. However, the Chancellor also decided that, because of the more selective nature of the proposed cuts, the Contingency Reserve ought to be increased under Option C by £2bn rather than the £1.5bn under Options A and B. In summary, the reduction in the planning total under Option C is £20bn, calculated as follows: £19bn (reductions in programmes) *plus* £3bn (central privatisation proceeds) *minus* £2bn (increase in Contingency Reserve).

The Star Chamber

The Cabinet was unable to agree upon the proposals put forward by the Chancellor, but did agree that discussions would proceed on the basis of Option C. Therefore, the Prime Minister appointed a Star Chamber, chaired by the Secretary of State for Energy, and which consisted also of the Foreign Secretary and of the Secretaries of State for Agriculture, Fisheries & Food and for Trade & Industry, as well as the Chief Secretary. The Chief Secretary eased the problem by volunteering a reduction of £3bn in the Contingency Reserve, provided that the Star Chamber then met the Chancellor's target. Advice had been given by the Chancellor that the £3bn privatisation target should be left at that level. The Chief Secretary emphasised his concern with the big numbers, and this shaped the decision on which ministers to interview: Health & Social Security, Employment, Defence, Scotland, Environment and Transport. Other ministers would have to appeal their case against the Star Chamber's decision direct to Cabinet: the Secretary of State for Energy set a good example by accepting his Option C figure.

The approach was inquisitorial, with the Chief Secretary firing the initial bullets at the spending ministers: one of his repeated themes was the Chancellor's generosity and an insistence that spending ministers should not be allowed to describe reductions against bids as cuts when there would still be real growth. The Secretary of State for Health Social Security came first, and was probed on a wide range of issues, some perhaps too detailed. Similar lengthy exchanges, often on programme detail rather than broad policy or expenditure trends, were repeated with the other ministers.

Table 3.3 records the recommendation of the Star Chamber with column 4 showing its programme allocations and column 5 the corresponding cuts against bids. Concessions of £500m were made to two of the big spending departments (Health & Social Security, and Defence) but the Star Chamber refused to budge on Employment despite a plea by the Secretary of State for Employment. The concession of £500m to Transport, whose Secretary of State strongly argued that his programme had the ability to generate useful genuine private sector jobs very quickly, owed much to the view that Employment had failed to convince colleagues that the route to higher employment was through subsidy schemes rather than programme expenditure. Environment recovered £500m after its Secretary of State had made a witty and telling attack upon centralised procedures. He stressed that the Cabinet certainly had the power to write expenditure plans on pieces of paper but simply could not - and he believed should not - deliver implementation on either level or composition, because much of the expenditure being discussed was actually the responsibility of separately elected local authorities whose decisions also cut across programmes.

Scotland recovered £500m on the argument that most of the Scotland programme is covered by an automatic (Barnett) formula which relates changes in Scottish expenditure to comparable changes in England. With information on exactly what was happening to comparable English expenditure not being available, the concession of £500m was intended to show recognition of this point. Trade & Industry's £500m owed much to that Secretary of State's position on the Star Chamber, and the fact that it wanted to secure a unanimous report. Because of the rush in which the Star Chamber was called upon to deliver its verdict after the ministers' appeals had been heard, and because of significant policy disagreements among its members, the actual numbers which emerged were strongly shaped by broad judgements and by assessments of political clout, much less on the merits of detailed arguments.

The final Cabinet meeting

Both the Prime Minister and the Chancellor pronounced themselves satisfied with the Star Chamber's recommendations, and the Prime Minister brushed off attempts to appeal against the verdict. However, the Chancellor announced his willingness, should his colleagues be agreeable, to cede £500m to Health & Social Security out of the

TABLE 3.3   THE STAR CHAMBER AND THE EVENTUAL DECISION FOR 1989/90

	Original Bids	Chancellor's Offer	Option C Cuts	Star Chamber Offer	Star Chamber Cuts	Eventual Decision
	£m	£m	£m	£m	£m	£m
Defence	22,375	19,875	(2,500)	20,375	(2,000)	20,375
Foreign & Commonwealth Office	2,204	1,970	(234)	1,970	(234)	1,970
Agriculture, Fisheries & Food	2,702	2,415	(287)	2,415	(287)	2,415
Trade & Industry	2,009	1,009	(1,000)	1,509	(500)	1,509
Energy	(300)	(500)	(200)	(500)	(200)	(500)
Employment	10,192	5,692	(4,500)	5,692	(4,500)	5,692
Transport	5,551	4,961	(590)	5,461	(90)	5,461
Environment	7,280	6,280	(1,000)	6,780	(500)	6,780
Home Office	6,476	5,788	(688)	5,788	(688)	5,788
Education & Science	17,424	16,424	(1,000)	16,424	(1,000)	16,424
Health & Social Security	71,964	67,964	(4,000)	68,464	(3,500)	68,964
Scotland	8,359	7,359	(1,000)	7,859	(500)	7,859
Other Departments	16,249	14,249	(2,000)	14,249	(2,000)	14,249
Total programmes	172,485	153,486	(18,999)	156,486	(15,999)	156,989
Contingency Reserve	9,750	11,750	2,000	8,750	(1,000)	8,250
Central privatisation proceeds		(3,000)	(3,000)	(3,000)	(3,000)	(3,000)
Planning total	182,235	162,236	(19,999)	162,236	(20,000)	162,236

Contingency Reserve in recognition of the good case which the Secretary of State had been putting up without very tangible success. The eventual decision on 1989/90 is thus shown in column 6 of Table 3.3. There was no time left at the weekend conference to take decisions on 1987/88 and 1988/89.

Comments upon the simulation

The Treasury ministers were pleased that they had protected the planning total with more success than might have been expected, especially in view of the significant relaxation in the real world climate towards public expenditure in the period after the simulation exercise had been designed. The announcement of the Autumn Statement figures (Treasury 1986c) on the eve of the November 1986 weekend conference gave spending ministers the option of claiming that they were being highly responsible. The simulation weekend finished with a 1989/90 planning total of £162.236bn compared with the £161.5bn figure emerging from the real Cabinet decisions (Treasury 1986c, 1987). The simulation incorporated a Contingency Reserve (which even after the last minute release of £500m to Health & Social Security) was £750m higher and central privatisation proceeds which were £2,000m lower. Programme expenditure in the 1987 White Paper (Cm 56, Treasury 1987) thus totalled £159bn whereas in the simulation it was £156.986bn.

Several striking features of the simulation deserve comment, some of which are echoed by spending ministers in Chapter 5. First, the spending ministers did an impressive job in complying with the Assessor's guidelines which formed the basis for the preparation of the Bid Book. Given the fact that specialist expertise in the programme area was the basis on which the spending ministers were chosen by the simulation Co-ordinator, this is perhaps not surprising. However, very few of them would previously have been subjected to the particular disciplines imposed by PESC. The weekend seminar itself became a little distorted in that arguments which ought to have been resolved between the Chief Secretary and the spending ministers spilled over into the full Cabinet. This problem was widely recognised and was directly the result of David Heald, who had prepared the guidelines and had made sure that they were understood, being in Australia for the whole period between the submission of the bids and the weekend conference itself. Otherwise, the idea had been that there would have been papers available tabling issues which had been agreed and which were still in dispute between the Chief Secretary and the spending ministers.

But, setting aside this logistical problem, it was striking that whereas ministers became skilled at performing the computational requirements of the guidelines, they found it virtually impossible to provide precise, rather than generalised, justifications of the cash increases. In particular, paragraph 4 of the guidelines had asked for distinctions to be made wherever possible between:

(i)   changes in the cost of providing the current level of service because of an increase in the number or mix of clients;

(ii)   increases in public sector costs above the projected change in the GDP deflator (the Relative Price Effect);

(iii)   policy changes; and

(iv)   other estimating changes.

Furthermore, departments were asked to make clear in their submissions both the part-year and full-year cost of changes. The difficulty which such distinguished programme experts found in providing even the crudest information of this sort is a telling indicator that, despite the sheer size of the current White Paper, much information relevant to policy choices is simply not published even when it is available.

The simulation Cabinet was inevitably less convincing than a real Cabinet, because political careers were not at stake nor was there a political agenda which would set a framework for priorities. What began as a heavily technocratic exercise, with ministers being for the most part academic programme experts, resolved itself very much by means of the exercise of personal authority and of crude horse trading. It was striking how little direct involvement in the detail there was either from the Prime Minister or from the Chancellor. Except at the Cabinet itself, the key protagonists were the spending ministers and the Chief Secretary. However, it was equally clear that the only reason why the revised planning total target was held was because of the personal authority of the Prime Minister and of the Chancellor. If there had been anything vaguely as democratic as a vote, the Chancellor's specification of the target planning total and his continual defence of the Contingency Reserve (and his active management of it as key tool) would have been overturned by his Cabinet colleagues. Similarly, there were occasions on which the Prime Minister suppressed challenges, and made it very difficult for ministers to continue their opposition.

The lack of a clear political agenda exhibited itself in several ways. There were occasions on which the Chancellor and the Chief Secretary found themselves in the ironic position of trying to protect certain programmes, even at the same time they were demanding very large cuts. For example, the Chancellor exempted Health & Social Security from his original list and surrendered £500m of the Contingency Reserve at the final Cabinet meeting. The Chief Secretary had inspired the (declined) offer in the Star Chamber to the Secretary of State for Health & Social Security, that he would receive an extra £1,000m provided he did not go back to Cabinet for more. Indeed, although Health & Social Security fared badly at the Star Chamber, it would probably have done worse but for the Chief Secretary. This was partly a result of the views of the members of the Star Chamber, the majority of whom were not sympathetic to the minister's claims, but also to the way in which that departmental budget absolutely dominates the planning total. It accounted for 39% of the original bids in the simulation. When attention turns to functional expenditure, thus bringing in the health and personal social services expenditure contained in the territorial programmes for Scotland, Wales and Northern Ireland, it accounted for 47% of the 1987 White Paper's planning total for 1989/90.

When there is a desperate search for savings, the contributions which can be made by smaller departments are necessarily small, and the big spenders are bound to be targets. The question therefore arises as to whether the two sides of Health & Social Security ought to be split, thus forming a Health Department for England and a Social Security Department for Great Britain (social security expenditure in Northern Ireland, pegged at the same rates of benefit, falls within the Northern Ireland programme). The tactic of putting small-spending ministers on the Star Chamber can reverberate, especially if they vigorously defend their own patch and extract concessions from the Chief Secretary who is predominantly anxious about the really big numbers.

There are several other issues deserving comment. The numerical calculations proceeded in terms of cash, but there is an understandable desire by spending ministers to conduct policy discussions in terms of an inflation-adjusted figure. Given the fact that ministers actually had limited information about both the likely outturn in the base year of 1986/87 and the specific rates of inflation relevant to their programmes, much of the argument about levels of service was very imprecise. This held true of discussions about inputs, even more so when any attempt was made to push the focus towards outputs. For all the recent discussion of performance indicators, the programme specialists playing the role of spending ministers found it very difficult to produce measures of output or performance which were capable of swaying opinion. The Secretary of State for Transport was unique in the emphasis he placed upon his department being able to generate cost-benefit rates of returns for his programmes. He also stressed that programme expenditure on transport was a cost-effective means of employment generation, but did not produce concrete numbers.

The crucial issue underlying much of the debate thus resolved into whether 'doing something' about unemployment necessarily meant giving more money to the Department of Employment. The controversy over how the Employment bid should be treated revealed complex divisions. Its sheer scale provoked hostility from the Chief Secretary. Moreover, the Treasury was insistent that the genuine efficiency gains secured during the harsh years for the public sector should not now be sacrificed through using the public sector as a mop for unemployment. In this, the Treasury found tacit support from the big spenders, like Health & Social Security, whose Secretary of State was alarmed at the implications of the extra ancillary staff which the Employment bid assumed would be absorbed into the National Health Service. Furthermore, there was no agreed basis for calculating what savings would accrue to the Health & Social Security budget for different levels of employment creation through the Employment budget. Paradoxically, this bid attracted most sympathy from those ministers who seemed to be least sympathetic to public expenditure in general. In the end, the view prevailed that the most desirable form of job creation through the public sector was to expand worthwhile programme expenditure. Nevertheless, the Secretary of State for Employment's claim that such measures would not tackle the problem of the long-term unemployed left some of those who had not been convinced by his proposals feeling somewhat uneasy.

Whether real-life Cabinet ministers would have been as keen to substitute asset sales for expenditure reductions would at least in part depend upon the political balance of that Cabinet. However, the numerical consequences for the declared planning total of the Treasury's practice of treating asset sales as negative expenditure have now assumed very great presentational significance. In the simulation, the £3bn central privatisation proceeds in 1989/90 made the target for trimming bids more manageable. However, as Table 3.4 vividly shows, this figure significantly underestimates the true size of privatisation proceeds for two reasons: the sales of land and buildings are kept outside the total for central privatisation proceeds; and the proceeds from the sales of assets by nationalised industries which are retained by them reduce the contribution which External Financing Limits make to

TABLE 3.4 THE TRUE CONTRIBUTION OF ASSET SALES TO THE PLANNING TOTAL, 1979/80 - 1989/90

	1979/80	1980/81	1981/82	1982/83	1983/84	1984/85	1985/86	1986/87	1987/88	1988/89	1989/90
	£m	£m	£m	£m	£m	£m	£m	£m	£m	£m	£m
Central privatisation proceeds	(377)	(405)	(493)	(488)	(1,142)	(2,132)	(2,702)	(4,750)	(5,000)	(5,000)	(5,000)
Sale of lands and buildings outside central privatisation proceeds	(878)	(1,316)	(2,139)	(2,860)	(2,462)	(2,441)	(2,566)	(2,841)	(2,650)	(2,600)	(2,650)
Asset sales proceeds retained by nationalised businesses	(240)	(215)	(216)	(318)	(230)	(430)	(206)	(76)	(300)	(250)	(200)
Total privatisation proceeds	(1,495)	(1,936)	(2,848)	(3,666)	(3,834)	(5,003)	(5,474)	(7,667)	(7,950)	(7,850)	(7,850)
Revised programme expenditure	79,055	94,575	106,835	117,135	124,153	134,780	139,096	148,217	153,075	156,550	161,850
Contingency Reserve									3,500	5,500	7,500
Adjustments								(150)			
White Paper planning total (Cm 56)	77,560	92,639	103,987	113,469	120,319	129,777	133,622	140,400	148,625	154,200	161,500

Notes: Privatisation proceeds have a negative sign. The entries for line 3 for 1985/86 and 1986/87 are unrevised and probably understated.

the planning total. The simulation certainly brought home that £8bn a year is a very large figure in the context of annual decisions on public expenditure!

Annex: The Simulation Planning Total

The Assessor's guidelines (see Annex B to Chapter 2) governed the preparation of the Bid Book. The guidelines provided for a 1987/88 planning total of £148.9bn; the simulation bids (see Table 7A of the Bid Book) came to £154.909bn, exceeding the guideline planning total by *£6.009bn* which therefore became the amount of cuts required if the target planning total was to be achieved for 1987/88. For 1989/90, the original bids totalled £182.235bn, *£24,035bn* above the guideline planning total of £158.2bn. Strictly following the guidelines, the cuts required in the respective years were the italicised figures.

However, the editors and the 'Chancellor' have to acknowledge an error in the early moves of the game which is perhaps not without counterpart in real-life Cabinet discussions. When the Co-ordinator prepared the Bid Book during the absence abroad of the Assessor, he made a different calculation, based on Table 7A of the Bid Book, which became the basis of the subsequent Cabinet discussions. This compared the 1989/90 bids with the 1986 White Paper figures for *1987/88*. He allowed a discretionary increase of '3 times £5bn' (£15bn) which was £10bn more than the guidelines had intended. On the other hand, the Co-ordinator did not allow for the normal expected price increase of, say, 3% for the transitions between 1987/88 and 1988/89, and between 1988/89 and 1989/90. Taken together, these omissions removed roughly £10bn of the £15bn global allowance. There were two other differences. He made no provision for privatisation proceeds whereas the Assessor had been willing to project these forward for an extra year at Cmnd 9702's level of £4.7bn; and he included in the planning total a higher Contingency Reserve (£9.75bn as against the Assessor's £8bn).

These events are a telling reminder of the importance of focusing upon the programme expenditure component of any given planning total. Naturally, spending ministers are primarily concerned to defend the programme bids which they submit.

1989/90, £bn	Assessor's guidelines	Bid Book	Eventual decision	Cm 56
Programme expenditure	154.900	172.585	156.986	159.000
Central privatisation proceeds	-4.700		-3.000	-5.000
Contingency Reserve	8.000	9.750	8.250	7.500
Planning total	158.200	182.235	162.236	161.500

4. Learning from Experience

Richard Rose and Phillip Davies

Anyone contemplating the dilemmas of public expenditure planning in the United Kingdom in the past decade is inclined to feel: 'There must be a better way'. A great advantage of being outside Whitehall is that one does not have to accept the rules of the game as it is played there. Yet anyone who wants to improve the workings of Whitehall must start with British government as it is. This constraint is particularly evident in public expenditure planning, for the process is not so much annual as it is continuous. The end of one year's cycle tends to overlap with the commencement of preparations for the next year.

A great advantage of a public expenditure simulation is that it allows people with knowledge of the problems of government to come to grips with the actual process of determining public expenditure, and of having decisions imposed by the pressure of events, colleagues and previous commitments. Just as it is easy for a saloon bar cricketer to explain how he would deal with a fast bowler in a Test Match, so it is easy for anyone to decide by himself or herself how public money ought to be spent. It is another thing altogether to get agreement around a Cabinet-size table, or to be satisfied with an agreement reached in a world where the inertia of established spending commitments is always great.

The first problem of a simulation is to identify the 'real world' which the simulation is meant to approximate. The obstacles to doing so are less the product of the Official Secrets Act, which screens information from those outside Whitehall, as they are the product of the misleading assumption that anything stated as a number is a constant. In the shadow world of negotiations about budget numbers, one can learn much about the inescapable problems of budgeting through collective decision-making. In addition, one can learn that even though whatever is may be thought right, it is not necessarily the only (or best) way to run the enterprise of British government.

In search of the actual budget

In order to evaluate the realism of a simulation, the first problem is to identify the actual budget. The first thing that we learn is that this is easier said than done. Some of the problems in focusing upon the most suitable numbers are technical: others are political.

The 1986 public expenditure White Paper (Cmnd 9702, Treasury 1986a), taken as our starting point, contains dozens of expenditure tables and each table has many different columns. The table of central importance for constraining departmental expenditure was Cmnd 9702's Table 2.1, *Planning total by department, 1978-79 to 1988-89*. The planning total is the global sum that the Treasury seeks to control in any given year. An increase in one departmental bid normally requires a compensating decrease in others, if the planning total is to remain constant.

Within this framework, any one of four years could be said to be the actual budget. If reality is defined in historical terms of what actually was spent, then the 1984/85 outturn was the latest year for which final figures were available in January 1986. For 1985/86 (i.e. the year ending on 31 March 1986), the figures to hand were estimates. A year later the Treasury showed that some of the plans for 1986/87 were well wide of the mark (by comparing Table 2.1 of Cmnd 9702-II with Table 2.1 of Cm 56-II). For example, Education & Science was underestimated by £1,635m; Social Security by £1,542m; and Health & Personal Social Services by £241m. Had we really been Cabinet ministers, more up-to-date information would have been available for the simulation than had been published. But ordinary MPs suffer under a similar disability to ours. The fundamental point remains valid: government data about what has already been spent can be unsatisfactory as a precise guide to planning ahead for some months after the financial year is over.

The extent to which official Treasury publications are unreliable guides to the future is even more striking. At the time of our simulation, the year ahead was 1987/88, starting on 1 April 1987. The published Treasury estimate of total expenditure in that year was £143.9bn (Cmnd 9702, Treasury 1986a). On the eve of the simulation, the Autumn Statement raised the planning total to £148.625bn (Treasury 1986c), later presented in more detail in the 1987 White Paper (Cm 56, Treasury 1987). Education & Science was up by £2,204m; Social Security by £1,602m; and Health & Personal Social Services by £673m.

The current budget year is a hybrid, consisting of both past and prospective figures. At the time of our simulation weekend in November 1986, half the financial year was over, and half was yet to come. Of course, there is considerable continuity from month to month in public expenditure. The base, the first £130bn or so of public expenditure, is thus certain. But since public expenditure decisions are about choices at the margin, then a £500m estimating error is a substantial sum, relatively and often absolutely.

In the literal sense, the future cannot be known for certain: only after the money is gone can we be certain of what was actually spent. The longer it takes to compile accurate information that updates no-longer-valid estimates, the more governments are in the position, as Harold Macmillan once remarked, of looking up information in last year's *Bradshaw*. The Treasury has made substantial steps over the years in keeping track of cash flows, and updating estimates, but 100% accuracy about expenditure is impossible to obtain within the current year. Moreover, the current year's expenditure is not the only year involved; the years ahead are also important.

Paradoxically, there is both too little and too much scope for political choice. There is too little choice, insofar as the differences between the published estimates and the actual expenditure reflect the impact of uncontrollables. Uncontrollables can be defined as those parts of the budget that cannot be altered by expenditure decisions, because they reflect statutory entitlements (e.g. pensions), contractual commitments (e.g. the salaries of established civil servants, or purchases of defence equipment), or other binding obligations (e.g. those arising from European Community membership). While the entitlements are fixed, the number of claimants is not. Social security spending rises when the number eligible to claim supplementary benefits and other statutory entitlements increases, as can easily happen with fluctuations in the economy.

There is too much scope for choice, insofar as any number that the Treasury publishes about future expenditure cannot be disproved, whether or not it appears reasonable. For example, the 1986 White Paper assumed that expenditure on Education & Science would remain virtually constant in cash terms from the 1985/86 estimated outturn (£14,461m) to 1988/89 (£14,470m). It could only do so by ignoring the existence of major negotiations concerning teachers' pay which accounts for the greatest single portion of that expenditure. Feeding this pay award into the calculations has significant consequences: the Department of Education & Science estimates the teachers' settlement for England and Wales as £779m in 1988/89 and £837m in 1989/90.

The Treasury accepts that its figures for departmental expenditure are not quite right by including a substantial reserve sum in its calculations for the year ahead. This Contingency Reserve, which is included in the planning total, it not committed to any one department, so it can be drawn upon subsequently as required, whether to fund increases arising from uncontrollables, or to fund measures that had been rejected at an earlier time but which now appear desirable or necessary on political grounds. Three months before the start of the 1986/87 financial year, the Treasury was still keeping a Contingency Reserve of £4.5bn, and this rose to £6.25bn for the year starting 15 months ahead, and £8bn to allow for contingencies in two years' time.

The reality of a budget is characterised by flux. At any given moment, say, at the date on which public expenditure totals are decided within Whitehall, the current official statement of expenditure is a fact. But because it is the product of an ongoing process, these 'facts' are not fixed. By the time the public expenditure White Paper is published months later, what is now the current figure is different. As circumstances fluctuate, numbers change. The budget is a set of variables. Expenditure numbers should be kept on a computer because this makes possible frequent and fast alteration in individual entries and in totals. A budget is constant only when it is dead, all the money having been spent, the figures having been audited, and the interest of the Treasury and spending departments having been redirected to the years ahead.

The simulation exercise was given dramatic evidence of the fluidity of the budget in the period between the first meeting in April 1986 and the weekend seminar in November 1986. At the initial meeting, it was agreed to simulate an increase in public expenditure. Considerable care was given to identifying what appeared a reasonable increase. In retrospect, our estimate looked too low, because on the day before our weekend simulation, the Chancellor of the Exchequer, Mr. Nigel Lawson, announced to the House of Commons an increase larger than we had allowed. Hence, our first lesson in adaptability was the need to adjust our spending limit upwards.

Learning about the inescapable

A group of experts in public policy, many with experience in Whitehall or Westminister, starts with one advantage and one disadvantage by comparison with ministers. The advantage was that each participant had spent many years concentrating specifically upon the policy area for which he submitted a departmental budget. By contrast, ministers are likely to change departments every two or three years, and usually are not experts on the substance of their department's policies.

Our disadvantage was that we were not experienced in the actual processes by which public expenditure is run within Whitehall. Drawing upon the expertise of a number of persons with experience made it possible to establish realistic rules of the game. Inevitably, these rules emphasised those features of budgeting that may not be regarded as attractive (such as the need to keep within a pre-agreed ceiling), but are nonetheless efforts to meet the constraints of government as it actually is. In carrying out the task of trying to reduce the gallons of budget requests to the quart containers available, each of us learned, or came to appreciate much more vividly, a number of inescapable features of budgeting in the United Kingdom. A catalogue of points vividly brought home by participating in a budget process includes the following.

Living with three elephants

Our normal picture of a Cabinet is of nearly two dozen different politicians, each with specific responsibilities, whether it be looking after foreign affairs, trade and industry, employment or Scotland. However, when a Cabinet is deciding on public expenditure totals, then half of the ministers are more or less on the sidelines, for they cannot be considered spending ministers. A few have a general interest in public expenditure because their job is to look after the government as a whole: this is particularly true of the Prime Minister. Others do have some money to spend, but in no sense is it a measure of their importance: for example, the Chancellor is not a big spender, nor is the Foreign Secretary.

Three departments are like elephants crowded into a tent designed for accommodating sheep, pigs, mules and other small-sized animals. Spending on Health & Social Security (44%), Defence (13%) and Education & Science (10%) together accounted for more than two-thirds

41

of Cmnd 9702's planning total for 1986/87. The White Paper's presentation of budgeted figures tends to minimise this point in two ways: it divides Health & Personal Social Services from Social Security, and spending on education and the social services outside England appears in the territorial programmes for Scotland, Wales and Northern Ireland, though their spending on social welfare more or less follows totals for England. Indeed, the total amount of money involved in these big programme headings is nearly three-quarters of UK public spending (74% of the functional analysis in Cmnd 9702's Table 2.12).

Any Chancellor who is to come to grips with public expenditure must address three ministries, and three ministers, none normally of senior Cabinet rank. The Chancellor cannot use his political standing to impose heavy cuts upon these ministries, for social policies are in the short term uncontrollable, and no government would casually repeal entitlements to major social benefits. Nor would a government casually introduce big cuts in defence because of the international repercussions. The Chancellor is far better positioned to prevent new programmes threatening large spending increases. Because these departments already claim so much public money, a 10% increase in their budgets would account for more than £9bn. Nor would other Cabinet ministers happily see billions going to a few middle-ranking Cabinet ministers, while their own department was being denied the few hundred millions that they sought.

None of the participants in the simulation exercise was so naive as to think that the whole of expenditure savings could be provided by altering the budget of a mythical Ministry of Waste. Nor was anyone shocked by the scale of marginal increases in a few big-spending ministries. What remains striking is the extent to which most spending ministers are, in sheer size of claims, junior players or spectators in the public expenditure game.

The meta-problem

A Prime Minister sees government as Winston Churchill saw puddings: a good pudding has a theme, and a bad pudding lacks one. There is a need for one or two guiding themes to give coherence to policy choices in many different areas. The theme may concern a single big issue, such as beating inflation, bringing down unemployment or defending the country. Or it may be no more than a tactical political goal: to win re-election. Whereas spending ministers tend to think narrowly, about matters principally of concern to their department, a Prime Minister must think big.

One aspect of the thematic approach to public expenditure is that themes tend to be expensive, in relation to the amount of money available at the margin each year. A big push on unemployment could easily cost £6bn to £10bn. A major push on Health & Social Security could cost as much as £15bn to £20bn. And a defence effort could slowly but surely build up to £10bn in increased annual commitments on equipment and personnel. When £5bn is considered a major increase and £10bn a very large increase - and cuts and zero growth years are also possible - it is fair to characterise a thematic priority as making a pre-emptive strike upon virtually all (or more than all) the discretionary money that the Treasury has. An intellectual case can be made for spending more money on caring for the sick, the elderly and the poor, just as a case can be made for doing something to bring down unemployment substantially. But both cases cannot be conceded by the Treasury at the same time because, within the tax limits maintained by successive Conservative and Labour Governments, the money is not there.

The simulation made clear the many difficulties in actually pursuing a thematic policy, or even in having a sustained collective discussion of the sort that might occur in a gathering of public-spirited citizens whose political careers and ministries were not at stake in the discussion. With a simulation Prime Minister stronger than some real occupants of the chair, public expenditure decisions avoided degenerating into a simple application of sharing pleasure and pain proportionately, giving each the same percentage increase. But they could not overcome the difficulties of discussing meta-problems, for the following substantial reasons.

Statutory programmes drive out novel proposals

In the bid for money, established programmes have two advantages. The first is that they are statutory commitments. Pensions, health care and education cannot be withdrawn insofar as they involve programmes for which benefits are mandatory. Secondly, established programmes have a track record of spending money. It is always uncertain what sum of money should be invested in a novel proposal. One way to resolve uncertainty is to give a novel programme a little. To give an untried and uncertain programme a large sum of money would show a willingness to run risks inconsistent with the Treasury's philosophy, and with that of most Prime Ministers.

The statutory expenditures of government can be estimated as claiming anything from 75% to 100% of last year's expenditure. For example, a department such as the Ministry of Agriculture, Fisheries & Food is not a big spending department in Whitehall terms, but the bulk of its expenditure is difficult to cut, since it is determined by European Community obligations. The Home Office is only middling in public spending, but cuts in spending would threaten such things as the police force, a move which few politicians would want to accept responsibility for.

Organised interests drive out unorganised interests

In a Cabinet, the ministries are the basic units of organisation, and discussion is structured in terms of ministers' interests, which are largely defined by the particular departmental brief of the moment. For example, there are always occasions when Scottish and Welsh concerns will be heard, because there are Secretaries of State for Scotland and for Wales in the Cabinet. Concerns of Yorkshire or of Greater London may not be addressed, because these territories do not have ministers. To give a politician ministerial status without a significant departmental budget would create a voice in the Cabinet, but it could not be followed by action in those areas where money talks.

In our simulation, Health & Social Security represented an organised interest, for it not only had an articulate minister but also a very large budget based on statutory entitlement. The unemployed, *per se*, had a minister whose departmental brief was both narrower and wider than the unemployed. The Department of Employment is concerned about creating and maintaining jobs, as well as doing something about the unemployed. But many of the actions that appear in lists of measures to fight unemployment would not be carried out by this department but by Trade & Industry and Education & Science or, in the field of macroeconomic policy, by the Treasury itself.

Little scope for thematic and strategic thinking

It follows from the above that while it is easy to organise a speech around a single theme, it is very difficult to organise a government or an expenditure process in such a way. The purposes of public expenditure are multiple and go off in many different directions.

In a more integrated system of government, such as the French Presidency when the Prime Minister was of the same party, it would be possible to conceive of a central agency of government providing thematic direction, acting under the authority of the President. In Washington, this is not possible because of the checks and balances restricting a President. In Whitehall, it is not possible because of the constraints of Cabinet government and individual ministerial responsibility, and the strict limits on the operational influence which 10 Downing Street can exert with a staff of only a few dozen. Whether a more presidential (i.e. heavily centralised and staffed) 10 Downing Street is desirable is debatable. What is indisputable at the moment is that any effort to characterise the spending priorities of British government is not likely to describe it as a pudding with a theme. It is more likely to appear a curate's egg, good in parts.

Worth further exploration

To accept that many features of the expenditure process cannot be changed does not mean surrendering to the fatalistic dictum: 'whatever is, is right'. The more one learns about a subject, the easier it is to discriminate between those things that must be accepted because they cannot be escaped, and those things that should be improved because they can be improved. Three points struck us as particularly offering scope for improvement, the first negative and the latter two positive.

Abandon the fiction of control

In continental languages, the word 'control' often refers to a process of verification or checking, or inhibiting. Mandarin English is exceptional in implying a sense of power, as in the phrase 'Treasury control'. But the power is not there. This is not only evident analytically, in terms of uncontrollable statutory commitments; it is also evident in practice, in a comparison of Treasury forecasts of what it will tax and spend, and what in fact happens (Mosley 1985). In relation to the power over events necessary to achieve fine tuning of the economy, including public expenditure, control is an aspiration rather than an achievement.

As a symbol, the doctrine of control obscures matters of importance. As George Jones argues in Chapter 6, a great deal of money that is notionally credited to ministers in the public expenditure exercise is actually spent by local authorities that have statutory obligations and powers to spend money. A systematic examination of spending ministries emphasises that this point is general: all but two of the spending ministries do not actually deliver the services for which they are responsible (Rose 1987, chapters 3 and 8). The Department of Education & Science does not run schools; the Department of the Environment builds no houses; and the Department of Energy does not operate nationalised industries. Local authorities, nationalised industries and bodies such as the National Health Service are the principal organisations delivering public services. The exceptions are the Ministry of Defence (although the uniformed services differ in significant ways from the civil service side) and the social security side of the Department of Health & Social Security, though the actual disbursement of some £40bn is thought so unimportant that it is put in the hands of an Under-Secretary in charge of a vast office in Newcastle-upon-Tyne.

There are two very different ways of altering the present curious half-way house of centralised expenditure discussions and fragmented service delivery. One would be to abandon the pretence that Cabinet ministers collectively do have their hands on the totality of public expenditure: this is the alternative that George Jones advocates. The other alternative is to centralise more responsibility for services within ministries, for example, by having the Department of Education & Science take over local education authorities and administer schools, along French lines.

Debt interest is omitted from the expenditure review on the grounds that it is notionally uncontrollable, though this accounted for £17.5bn in 1986/87 (Cm 56, Table 2.20, Treasury 1987). If there were to be a Minister for Debt Interest, that person could claim to be one of the Cabinet's biggest spenders, and certainly in charge of what has been one of its fastest growing expenditure items. Whilst debts cannot legally be repudiated, the actual interest paid is variable, and government policy on monetary and other matters is directly relevant to the actual cost of debt interest. Because debt interest is a first charge upon public funds, payments made under this heading limit the amount of tax and other revenue available to finance programmes within the planning total. The pressures to prevent debt interest from rising have a knock-on effect upon taxation as well, requiring substantial taxation to fund debt interest, or inhibiting tax cuts financed by increased borrowing.

In a period of slow growth in the economic base funding public expenditure and continued pressures to spend more, governments in all OECD countries have faced the problem of 'doing something' about public expenditure. OECD itself has organised a major study of the many things attempted, with widely varying degrees of failure or success: for example, impose global ceilings in total spending; modify indexation; decentralise the process of cuts; improve cash flow management; introduce new constitutional rules; and provide incentives for retrenchment (see, for example, Tarschys 1985). From a vast menu of possibilities, two may be noted here.

(i)   envelope budgeting

> Public expenditure is a process of negotiation, because it is necessary to match the Treasury's proper concern with global sums in the budget and the responsibilities of spending ministries for particular budget lines. The present method for reconciling differences involves Star Chamber meetings, in which major spending ministers give judgements about the difficult issues that spending ministers persist in pursuing. The logic is simple: disinterested ministers judge interested ministers. This is consistent with the hallowed Whitehall dictum that amateurs are ultimately better judges than professionals. But another view can be taken, which is consistent with normal management practice outside Whitehall, namely, that those who know most about a subject are likely to be the best judge of problems and best able to decide allocations within limits. In short, professionals should judge themselves, and negotiate with similarly positioned professionals.
>
> Envelope budgeting is a concept that applies this philosophy, by dividing total expenditure into several large envelopes, with sums determined by the Treasury. Each envelope represents a functional area of government, for example, social welfare or industry or economic affairs. The ministers for each broad function are asked to take decisions about which programmes will be funded at the margin subject to the overriding authority of the government collectively. In this way, Health, Personal Social Services, Social Security and Education & Science may negotiate with each other about how money might best be added or subtracted in social policy. Trade & Industry, Energy

and Transport could negotiate about industrial and economic problems, and so forth. As long as each group was held to its overall total, the overall structure of the budget would be unaffected; the details would be decided by those who know and care, rather than by a mixture of amateurs and professionals.

(ii)   virement

A more radical change would be to extend the principle of virement, that is, the authority to transfer significant sums of money between programmes within each spending department. A minister who was sure that any savings he found through cuts would be at his disposal to apply to programmes that in his judgement were worth more money would have greater incentives to find cuts. At present, funds saved through cuts go back to the Treasury's central pool. The present system provides sticks but not carrots for ministers to make cuts, and it gives them no discretion in showing, by actions taken on their own, where they think money could best go.

Money isn't everything

One of the striking features of the simulation is that the majority of proposals for increased spending (or reductions in spending) involved relatively small sums of money (see Table 7B of the Bid Book). The median bid for more money asked for was £23m, equivalent to a 0.015% increase in total public expenditure: and 0.5% of the £5bn initially made available in the simulation for increased public expenditure. The mammoth bids were few, and predictably came from such places as the Department of Health & Social Security. Moreover, the simulation reflects the changes that actually take place in Whitehall each year.

To note how relatively little is required to make many ministers happy - at least about a few matters - is not to deny that money matters in government. The idea that government could be run without big taxes or by providing spiritual values is inconsistent with government as we have known it in the United Kingdom since 1940 and before.

The relevant point here is: how much do many of these small sums matter to the government, and to the economy as a whole? Even more, how much do they matter to the Treasury? And what is the nature of the Treasury interest? If the Treasury's interest in programmes is principally a matter of public finance, then any system of budgeting should be acceptable to it, as long as it stayed within the parameters of public spending that it is authorised to lay down. If its interest is in management and the efficiency of programmes, then it will have to make big changes within itself, in order to develop the expertise and sustained competence to evaluate and advise, or to understand the details that concern programme experts.

The fact that some programmes do not cost large amounts of money does not mean that they are necessarily unimportant or uninteresting to the minister responsible, the staffs producing them, or the people enjoying their benefits. At a time when British government necessarily must impose tight constraints upon the big spending programmes, then there is some reason to consider ways in which, within these constraints, more flexibility can be introduced. This will lighten the load of a centre already suffering from overload (as much a function of lack of time and knowledge as of excess of demand), and also offer greater scope for those in charge of smaller programmes and public agencies to seek satisfactions that, within their compass, appear big.

5. Reflections of Spending Ministers

Ministry of Defence: *David Greenwood*

My initial submission was an example of the 'camel's nose' tactic: an unexceptionable bid for 1987/88 (7% increase on the previous year, representing a 'fair share' of the new money available), heralding more contentious claims for 1988/89 and 1989/90 (based on the notion of restoring 3% real growth in the defence budget year-on-year, in line with NATO ministers' resource guidance). Even so I was surprised that, as the first stage of the exercise, the Chancellor axed the bid for 1989/90 (his focal year) by no less than £3.5bn, arguing that Defence had enjoyed a good run in the competition for resources in previous years and should now be limited to level funding in cash terms. What did not surprise me was that the major social spending departments concurred in his judgement.

Needless to say, I protested at the unjustifiably harsh treatment of my bid and pointed out the consequences of the reduction proposed (using arguments based on the material presented in my initial bid, viz. that the Trident programme would be at risk, together with desirable modernisation plans of the nation's contributions to NATO's conventional order of battle). I mentioned also that our allies, including the United States, would be strongly critical of our cavalier rejection of NATO's 'resource guidance': an argument for which I expected support from the Foreign and Commonwealth Office, but surprisingly (and unrealistically, I think) received none.

At our second session with the Chancellor, I was gratified to find £1bn 'restored' to my programme. But I wanted more. I decided not to plead but to declare that I could 'live with' this allocation, on the grounds that with window-dressing we could claim to be working towards resumption of 3% real growth. At the same time, however, I advised colleagues that, within the Ministry of Defence, we would, of course, have to explore the consequences of terminating the Trident programme; consider how to limit the damage to our standing in NATO that would result from diminution of our contributions to the Alliance's conventional forces in the Eastern Atlantic and Western Europe; and work out what forces in the

United Kingdom might now have to be reduced or disbanded. Under this last heading, I warned colleagues that among the items for which continuing provision would be in question were the Royal Yacht, the Queen's Flight and the Army's so-called public duties battalions (which might evoke protests from the Palace), plus RAF communications/transport aircraft for ministerial use (which could inconvenience them). More generally, I brought to colleagues' attention the fact that with the funding proposed we would, of course, no longer be able to regard ourselves as a military power on a par with France and the Federal Republic of Germany but, rather, as in the same league as, say Italy.

In the Star Chamber proceedings I indicated where the £2.5bn 'savings' now sought against my original bid for 1989/90 would have to be found:

	£m	
Nuclear strategic forces	750	cancel Trident
Navy general purpose forces	500	sell an aircraft carrier; pay off some older ships; build fewer new ones
European theatre ground forces and RAF general purpose forces	1000	cut force levels; stretch/cancel re-equipment plans
Home base forces	250	Royal Yacht etc.
	2500	

I then reiterated my reservations about the wisdom of retrenchment on this scale. Wishing to be constructive, I proposed that it would be more reasonable to seek a cut of, say, £1.4bn in the 1989/90 figure for Defence (to give an allocation of £21bn). That could be achieved, I suggested, by cancelling Trident (£750m) - for which I offered to construct a rationale based on the 'new atmosphere' for arms control - and by selected economies elsewhere (£650m). What the Star Chamber decided in effect was to 'split the difference' between the cut sought by the Chancellor (£2.5bn) and that which I had offered (£1.4bn). They did stipulate, however, that Trident should *not* be cancelled. Thus, Defence ended up with an allocation of £20,375m for 1989/90 (or £2bn less than my original bid) *and* instructions to find the necessary 'savings' in the non-nuclear parts of the programme.

All things considered, I was reasonably satisfied with the financial outcome: I think I fought my corner competently (and fared slightly better than my 'real life' counterpart in the 1986 survey round). I was less happy with the Trident stipulation, not least because I do not believe that colleagues made it on the basis of a thorough discussion of the priority to be accorded to strategic nuclear forces vis-a-vis a comprehensive and balanced contribution to NATO's conventional strength.

Foreign & Commonwealth Office: *William Wallace*

I was asked for 'a brief reflection' on how I felt I had handled my ministerial case. I can only be brief; the overwhelming impression which I got out of the seminar is what relatively small parts low-spending departments like the Foreign & Commonwealth Office play in an overall spending review. There is a natural tendency therefore for the Treasury to impose percentage cuts on all smaller spending departments, unless there is sufficiently strong political pressure to make an exception. Meanwhile, the major battles go on around the major spending departments.

In retrospect, what I should have done if I wished to buck the trend would have been to put a very strong case for a major new initiative. But it would have had to come with prime ministerial backing to be successful; in order to 'make waves' of the sort which Health & Social Security or Environment can manage, the percentage increase would have had to be enormous.

The smaller spending departments are therefore enormously dependent upon the broader context for public spending reviews: commitments in the manifesto, unanticipated new developments in domestic or external politics, prime ministerial preferences, or strong opposition pressure. These were not, in the nature of the exercise, built into this simulation. As several of us remarked at the end, it would have been useful to have had a 'manifesto' document as part of the context for the simulation; for those concerned with the politics of the public spending exercise, manifestos, like prime ministerial speeches, provide pegs on which to hang demands.

Department of Agriculture, Fisheries & Food:
Allan Buckwell

Despite the rather cynical rebuttals by the Prime Minister to the effect that the ideological stance of the average Cabinet is indistinguishable from that of any random collection of intelligent people, I do believe that our simulation suffered from a lack of commitment to any clear stand on the general desirability of more or less public expenditure. Likewise, the fact that we had not fought an election campaign in which we had or had not made clear commitments to major issues such as plans to reduce significantly the numbers of long-term unemployed, or the scrapping of Trident, made the discussions on these big issues rather empty.

Thus, to my mind, our discussions on the big expenditure increase on employment creation, which was the only really radical proposal in the whole exercise got lost in the complete lack of commitment by the Cabinet. With hindsight, those of us who felt strongly about this did not marshal the arguments with sufficient vigour, nor did we get together to lobby informally on the proposals. These omissions were partly due to the artificiality of the exercise in which none of us knew each other nor our views. There was thus too little time to create cabals and pressure groups.

The other major shortcoming of our simulation was that we were insufficiently briefed on the spending programmes of other departments. This was a consequence of selecting for the exercise people who were very knowledgeable about their own programmes but who were more than usually ignorant (compared to experienced, senior Cabinet members) of programmes in other areas. This problem became most apparent in the Star Chamber exercise in which we were unable significantly to dent any of the ministers because of a lack of good ammunition. I assume that in reality this ammunition would be provided both by the Treasury and the sheer experience of the kind of people normally on the Star Chamber.

On my own programme, I went along with the decision of the Cabinet to cut my expenditure, but totally without conviction. The decision had no real content because the bulk of the expenditure is out of the control of the UK budgetary process. In reality, I would hope that a Cabinet did not blind itself by taking decisions which it knew perfectly well it had zero chance of implementing. This posed a tactical problem for me because, as Minister for a very small spending department, it seemed unreasonable to take up Cabinet time over small and tediously complex programmes. Yet, if everyone took this attitude, the large sum of many, individually small, programmes could fall outside the process.

On another specific issue, I went away thinking that we had let the Secretary of State for Health & Social Security browbeat us into accepting that £8bn of the £11bn extra funds he was bidding for were absolutely inviolable. If we had not agreed the rather generous increase in global expenditure initially, he would have been making just as powerful a case about a much smaller amount. The lesson I took from this is that, as in many joint decision-making processes, he who is prepared to pursue an issue longest wins.

Finally, I did not feel the observers contributed much to the proceedings. The one kind of input which was lacking, yet I feel could have provided important insights, was that of behavioural scientists. We were apparently more concerned with the substance of the decisions than the process. Experts in group decision-making and group dynamics could have been useful. This would be particularly true if the exercise were repeated for aspiring Cabinet ministers or politicians.

Department of Energy: *Graham Hadley*

Taking account of my proposals for modest increases in departmental expenditure, in 1989/90 (the year upon which Cabinet discussion focused) my Department was the only one making a negative contribution to the public expenditure total. Broadly speaking, in that year, departmental expenditure of approximately £700m would be more than offset by net receipts from the nationalised energy industries of about £1bn (including borrowing by British Coal of £200m and repayments by the electricity supply industry of £1.2bn), thus leaving, overall, a net payment of £300m to the Exchequer.

I was able to respond positively to the Chancellor's proposal that my Department should make a further £200m contribution to the Exchequer in 1989/90 which I would meet through undertaking to reduce or eliminate the Redundant Mineworkers' Pension Scheme. There is of course some risk that a significant reduction in these payments will have the effect of slowing down labour cost reductions in the coal industry and thus increasing British Coal's EFL but I shall explore with it ways of ensuring that costs continue to reduce, so that it remains on target for the eventual elimination of subsidy.

It was proposed that receipts in 1989/90 should be increased by £3bn through privatisation and the Central Electricity Generating Board was identified as a possible candidate. Colleagues agreed, however, that it was in fact possible to score £3bn in 1989/90 against this heading without at this stage clearly identifying the source or sources given that there remain quite a number of potential candidates within the public sector including Regional Water Authorities, British Steel, the Post Office and the profitable parts of British Coal and British Rail as well as the electricity supply industry. In practice, in order to achieve receipts from sale of part of the electricity supply industry in 1989/90 a very early start on legislative proposals would be required because privatisation of this industry poses structural and other political problems, the solution of which will require careful planning. The principal problems involve future responsibilities for the construction and operation of nuclear power stations; and the question of obligations which privately owned electricity undertakings might, or might not, have to purchase coal from British Coal.

As a minister whose departmental programmes were not substantially affected by the debate about spending in 1989/90, I was glad to chair the Star Chamber which was able to recommend to Cabinet a package of reductions in departmental bids which met the Chancellor's requirement for a £20bn cut. The Star Chamber took the view that since this result would still leave total public expenditure approximately £18bn up on the base year, with each major spending department enjoying a share of the increase across a spread of programmes, the overall economic climate would not justify a failure to achieve the target set by the Chancellor. The proposals were accepted by the Cabinet.

Department of Employment: *Mark Cornelius*

The chief aim of my Department in the last public expenditure round was to secure funding for a radical and ambitious programme to ease the most pressing economic and social problem which this country faces, namely long-term unemployment. My proposal was to provide the guarantee of an offer of a job to all 1.3 million long-term unemployed people. My arguments in Cabinet were as follows. Either through employer choice or their own demoralisation, the long-term unemployed had almost ceased to be part of the effective labour force. In other words, they would be the last to benefit from any general recovery in the economy. However, on humanitarian grounds it would be fairer to give the long-term unemployed priority as they had endured the most suffering. Moreover, because the long-term jobless were effectively not competing with the short-term unemployed for jobs they no longer exerted any downward pressure on wage inflation. Thus, an attempt to reduce long-term unemployment would not risk setting in motion an inflationary upsurge, as perhaps would an attempt to reduce unemployment generally.

Despite the political differences of my Cabinet colleagues on many other issues, it became clear that the reduction in unemployment was an important priority. However, my colleagues made much of the fact that their own departments would be creating jobs if they were allowed to spend more and there was a worry that the jobs my programme would create were not real. I continued to stress that targeting towards the long-term unemployed was important, for the reasons already mentioned, and that the jobs I was proposing to create were real, in the sense that the people recruited for them would be doing necessary work alongside normally recruited workers in an ordinary working environment.

In the end, I feel (or hope) that my colleagues must have accepted some of what I said as I received a £2bn increase over my Department's expenditure in 1986/87: the largest proportional increase, I believe, of any department.

Department of Transport: *Stephen Glaister*

When thinking about the strategies that I might use when preparing my bid I identified three features of Transport public expenditure which I might be able to exploit. First, and most important, the analysis of rates of economic return to public expenditures is particularly well-developed for transport, partly because the subject is amenable to this kind of analysis and partly because economists have striven to make their voices heard with more success in this area than in some others. As a result, it is possible to back up claims about what the extra money would buy both in the physical sense and in the sense of economic benefit. Second, the share of Transport in the public budget has been falling steadily while the demand for most of the services that it provides are well known to have been growing rapidly. Hard evidence is becoming available that the pigeons are on their way back to roost. Third, Transport is a small and therefore fairly invisible department. If my bid was modest then there was a fair chance that it would not attract much attention when the cutting back of bids began.

I had a further reason for not putting in a bid for a very large increase. The rules announced in advance had not declared a discipline against the ploy of gross over-bidding purely in order to be able to offer many items for sacrifice and yet end up with a larger allocation. I anticipated that the Chancellor and his Assessor would find a way of punishing such an obvious ploy, should it be used, in order to prevent it from distorting the outcome. With these points in mind I put together a modest bid which it would be possible to defend in detail on the strength of evidence about economic rates of return. Of course, I did include one or two thinly-disguised hostages which could be sacrificed without too much pain when cuts were asked for.

In Cabinet the strategy worked much as I had hoped. The hostages were duly given up but I was left with a very much smaller cut from my original bid, both absolutely and proportionately, than any other department. In fact a degree of underspend on the proposed extra expenditure on new roads (some of which would be likely for administrative reasons) would probably allow me to undertake most of the proposals in my original bid.

I have the following observations on the events in Cabinet. The initial punishment of over-bidding that I had anticipated did not in fact occur. The Chancellor's first move was to total the bids and suggest approximately equiproportional cuts to bring the total back to what was available. This had several unfortunate consequences. First, large and weakly justified bids were allowed to distort both the discussions and the eventual outcome. A second consequence was that we were immediately in conflict with one another, seeking to defend our own department at the expense of some other. This meant that we never had the opportunity to consider as a collective Cabinet which of the new initiatives contained in the various bids were worthwhile. Since the talk was all of cuts - rather than of how additional money might be well spent - any imaginative new proposal became a target. I regretted this since I would have liked to have given some of the ideas a better run, particularly those from Employment, the Home Office, and Trade & Industry. At a late stage a proposal was made that this deficiency be repaired by reverting to consideration of equiproportional increases on White Paper expenditures. Although my own Department would have done less well out of this I felt it was a shame that the proposal was rejected so summarily.

It emerged in discussion that one 'policy' that the Cabinet as a whole would support would be using the additional expenditure to alleviate unemployment. There were at least three suggestions around the table as to how this might be done: direct creation and guarantee of jobs (Employment); subsidy to private sector employers (Trade & Industry); and increased purchase of commodities by spending departments, generally so as to preserve the infrastructure, (Transport, for example). It interested me that we were able to argue the merits of our respective 'solutions' purely on the basis of assertion. When asked if I thought that building roads was an effective way of increasing employment I was allowed to assert that it was better than creating 'paper jobs'. But I could never have defended that assertion on the basis of evidence. I imagine that the Star Chamber had considerable difficulty in resolving the question on the basis of anything other than guesswork.

Further, I was conscious of a lack of any reasoned collective view as to how an employment policy, if successful, might affect the demands made on particular departments - less still on how it might affect Exchequer revenue had that been thought to be a relevant consideration. As an observer pointed out, big issues which are difficult to research (for instance, the overall impact of government policy on income distribution) can become important quite quickly. In these circumstances, it must be difficult for a Cabinet to formulate a reasoned strategy while reconciling the conflicting interests of individual departments.

I knew from the beginning that the insistence on working with cash estimates would cause confusion at some point because of the failure to abstract from inflation. It was not until the exercise was over that I really understood where this had occurred. In the closing stages it became apparent during negotiation with Health & Social Security that there was some peculiarity. In retrospect it is easy to see that the increase in the Contingency Reserve in 1989/90 (which we had all noted) was so large that even after the Chancellor had agreed to reduce it somewhat, the increase available to departments over the White Paper figure for 1986/87 was only very slightly more than enough to cover expected inflation. Since the total had to stay roughly constant in real terms, a large department like Health & Social Security which had very reasonably held benefits constant in real terms, would impose substantial real cuts on other departments compared with 1986/87 if it was allowed to budget for real pay increases and other additional expenditures. Inflation obscured this simple truth. I suspect that if it had been clearly perceived at the time that we were really considering standing still in real terms (even before any real pay increases), then the overall outcome would have been different. In particular, I doubt if Transport would have been able to defend the substantial real increase that it in fact achieved. One of the observers was quite right to point out that our initial bids and our subsequent debates both failed to give adequate attention to either relative price effects or the overall effects of inflation.

Department of the Environment: *George Jones*

A sponsoring minister can get away with radical cuts in his programmes, and make major changes of priority within the given total. Increases from previous years are scrutinised, but big increases can be achieved if a huge initial bid is put in. There is no incentive to be economising in the initial bid. It is impossible for a small group at the centre to make trade-offs between such a vast and complex set of variables and to have control over them. Because the centre is so overloaded the answer is to seek more manageable government, first by removing local government spending financed by local taxation from the PESC process and then by instituting decentralisation.

The Chancellor queried the consequences of the abolition of the urban programme specific grant. I pointed out that it went on such bodies as the Rastafarians, grants to local authorities such as Hackney and Islington, and to programmes best suited for the budgets of other departments, like new factories, highway access, crime prevention, under-fives provision, and anti-drug efforts. Either, then, other departments should do these themselves, or better, allow local authorities the freedom to decide what to do. He queried the effect of reducing subsidies on council house rents. It could be rent increases of £2-3 per week, but in any case it is important for tenants to realise the real cost of their housing. These increases in rents would only entail increases in the Health & Social Security budget if the present subsidy system remains in place. For the sake of realism, they should revise it. I promised to support the Chancellor in abolishing mortgage tax relief. I emphasised that the increase in housing capital spending was not so much an increase in activity as an attempt to avoid a cut. It is to preserve the level of 1986/87, which is itself well below the level of 1981/82. A similar point is relevant also to the cash increase in local environmental services capital. All this capital spending represented real jobs in building industry.

I pointed out that, unlike other ministers, I had made cuts in departmental administration. When the Chancellor insisted on cuts of £1,000m, I protested that he had not made his priorities clear. He seemed to have penalised those departments which had made a real effort to cut and had given much bigger increases to departments which had put in the most excessive bids. He had given no incentive to economy. After cross-examination in the Star Chamber, I was given a revised cut of £500m. Although protesting, I showed my willingness to play with the team and dutifully made cuts to the exact amount:

		£m
7.1	subsidies for revenue deficits	311
8.2	local environmental services	47
8.6	environmental research	20
8.1	nationalised industries' EFLs	30
8.9	public corporations - Urban Development Corporations	52
	- New Towns	40
		500

I justify these cuts as a necessary means of avoiding significant cuts in capital spending. They entail phasing out rent subsidies at a faster rate than I had originally intended: realism will be attained sooner rather than later. Local environmental services have had to experience the minimum cut possible while keeping to the target. Environmental research has had to be cut; there is much doubt about its value: the money may be largely spent on white-coated academics playing with theories. We can pick up the findings of research from elsewhere more cheaply. The need for nationalised industries' EFLs can be eliminated either by water privatisation or by pushing up water charges. The Urban Development Corporations can be phased out more quickly than I had earlier intended, and we can speed up the sale of New Town assets.

Home Office: *Nicholas Deakin*

Generally, it seemed to me that my programme fared badly in Cabinet. This may have been something to do with the way in which it was presented, but essentially I think that my failure can be attributed to the type of programme that I was advocating. This was right in the general sense of being innovative and radical, but wrong for the type of exercise that we were conducting, in that radical elements did not take the form of drastic expenditure changes. Thus, the type of issue that I was trying to advance did not provide me with leverage in the kind of discussion that actually took place. With hindsight, I would have done better to stick to an incremental programme and argue around specific small-scale changes in existing policies. As a postscript, the one issue on which I did engage Cabinet's interest - the privatisation of prisons - has suddenly become very topical. If this had occurred a month earlier then I would have had a much stronger handle for raising radical questions about policy objectives.

I felt that I had done better in Cabinet than other ministers. I saw clearly what the Chief Secretary was trying to do, and tried then to mount a challenge. Once we had got to the Star Chamber stage, of course, it was impossible to derail the locomotive and the second attempt to mount a challenge was doomed to failure.

More generally, I continue to regret the omission of a political dimension in our discussions. If the exercise is repeated, a Chief Whip and a manifesto are essential ingredients not just in order to preserve reality, but in order to shake off the excessively technocratic flavour which I think we all observed.

Department of Health & Social Security:
Michael O'Higgins

The dominating effect of the way the Health & Social Security bid was treated by Cabinet colleagues was the effect of its sheer size. Taking almost half of all public spending, any increase in its budget was bound to appear excessive. In some ways, this caution is proper: the extent to which public spending is successfully planned or controlled is strongly affected by similar success or failure in respect of Health & Social Security spending. But the format adopted for discussing the bids suffered, I think, from two weaknesses which overstated the effective size of my bid for extra resources:

(i)   the starting point was planned rather than outturn spending; and

(ii)   'standstill' costs were not distinguished from 'growth' costs.

The estimated outturn for 1986/87 was some £800m greater than the plan in the bid; in reality, the difference is almost £1.5bn. The presentation of bids by the secretariat and by the Chief Secretary as growth on 1986/87 plan therefore overstated the actual increase being sought, and thus distorted the choice facing the Cabinet.

In a situation where participants will not be aware of the details of other budgets, it would be useful to distinguish 'standstill' from 'growth' costs, so that non-specialists can tell at a glance whether (say) increased pension spending is because of inflation-uprating or greater numbers of pensioners on the one hand, or real benefit improvements on the other. This is not to argue that overshoots on plan or increased 'standstill' costs should automatically be conceded, but that more explicit and better-understood decisions would be possible if these distinctions were made. Any attempt to distinguish standstill from growth costs in this fashion would require a specification of what the standstill level of service actually is - something which is not totally straightforward in the case of health or social service levels, nor in the case of other public services. Nonetheless, such an effort would be worthwhile as a contribution to discussion on the costs of maintaining current levels of service.

These features of the organisation of the discussion go some way towards explaining why my bid in this simulation exercise fared less well for 1989/90 than the Department itself in the Autumn Statement. There are two further reflections on this. First, Health & Social Security will undoubtedly claim a significant share of the large Contingency Reserve maintained by the Treasury in this simulation - not least because of its demand-led programmes, spending on which will inevitably be underestimated in consequence of the lower allocation received.

Second, the Health & Social Security bid suffered from a tactical error in my presentation, in that no concessions were offered at the Star Chamber stage of the exercise. To some extent, I treated this more akin to bilateral negotiations where one tests to find what the real spending limits might be. Some concessions at that point, coupled with further argument about why further concessions would involve service or benefit cuts, might have led to more sympathetic treatment by the Star Chamber.

Like the other participants to whom I have spoken, I found the exercise fascinating not simply for the two days of collective decision-making, but also for the earlier stage of having to cost and project forward the alterations one might want to make to a spending programme.

Scotland: *James Ross*

I would like to record comments on two issues; the handling of the Scottish bid, and the general conduct of the simulation.

The decision to include in the exercise a bid for the services within the responsibility of the Secretary of State for Scotland was taken fairly late. I doubt whether the inclusion of Scotland was necessary, and I think only one point of interest for the conduct of this exercise, and any others similar, arises from the handling of the Scottish bid.

There was an imbalance of expertise around the table. Territorial and functional departments probably do not call for any different techniques of decision-taking - and techniques of decision-taking were the point of the exercise. But they do raise rather different considerations. If emphasis, interest and knowledge of the various issues for decision are not well balanced among those deciding, the decision-taking process is likely to be distorted even if, nominally, the same techniques are applied to all issues.

It was evident that, whereas there was great knowledge and commitment on all the functional subjects, only three people knew or cared anything about Scotland. One of these was myself and one of the others was precluded by his role from any active participation in the debates about the cuts to be applied to each bid. The remaining participants appeared to work on a preconception that Scotland had been much too generously treated in the past and that this should be put to rights at once. Neither the specifics of the Scottish bid nor the basics of regional policy were ever discussed. I could certainly have done more to enlighten people, but only at a cost to the general balance of the exercise, which did not stand to gain much, if anything, from the better handling of the Scottish bid alone. I ought, however, to record certain points about the handling of the bid.

There is a mixture of reasons for the historic pattern of Scottish expenditure; the specific circumstances of Scotland, the generalised needs of disadvantaged regions, the nature of the response of central government to the political necessity of at least seeming to try to equalise prosperity between regions, and the effectiveness of Scottish government in exploiting all of these. The discussion, and the decisions of the Star Chamber and the Chancellor, took exaggerated account of the last factor and no account of the others.

In the review discussion after the exercise, I pointed out that, if there were a case for the reduction of Scotland's share of public expenditure, the reduction would be effected gradually by formula. However, no Secretary of State for Scotland could be expected to suggest such a formula. He could not afford politically to allow his name to be associated with a formula designed to make Scotland progressively worse off in relative terms. Such formulae have to come from Treasury ministers.

Turning to the wider issues, the simulation proceeded on the basis that:

(a)   there must be a better way of doing the job than the one currently adopted; and

(b)   we should tackle the job of finding the better way by initially following the existing procedure.

I do not dispute (a) but I do dispute (b).

Any simulation following existing procedure must do so inefficiently. This is because, whatever the expertise of the participants, it cannot reproduce the structure of long-term relationships and pre-consultations that act as a foundation for ministerial input under the present procedure. Any simulation working from existing procedure is therefore dependent on an early perception of some relatively fundamental flaw in the existing procedure. However, any such flaw is likely to have been suggested by prior academic study. It would therefore seem best to start the simulation on the basis of testing improvements conceived by academic study.

In practice, with one exception which I mention below, no significant improvements were suggested at the simulation, or seem to arise readily from it. I exclude the proposal to leave local government locally-funded expenditure out of account on the ground that, whatever its merits as a public finance practice, it does not affect the techniques or quality of decision-making on whatever is comprehended by government expenditure.

I suggest that, in this context, the Public Finance Foundation reflects on how much scope there now is for improvement of procedures as against change of organisation. Metaphorically, the British government engine is now of very venerable design. It is a tribute to the original design that it has proved capable of so much development over so long a period. But I think we must ask how much more horsepower we can realistically expect to extract from this decidedly old-fashioned set of working parts. We should also remember that those running the engine are not fools, except maybe in their attachment to it. If it could yield more power, they would probably have managed that by now.

It was suggested in the course of the simulation that a more coherent result might emerge from a more centralised process of decision, whereby the Prime Minister, possibly along with the Chancellor, took and promulgated the decisions, all other ministers being then required to make the best of them. I make no comment on the general merits or demerits of such a procedure. But the countries where it happens at present are politically and otherwise structured quite differently from the United Kingdom. Before one speculates about such a procedure, or tests its qualities by simulation, one would need to ask whether it could work efficiently, or at all, within existing British structures.

6. Postscripts

Performance appraisal: *Ian Beesley*

The discussion of departmental bids raised the fundamental issue of how to probe the great mass of on-going public expenditure. What seemed to be needed was an approach which would stimulate policy managers within departments to seek further ways of improving performance against budget as a matter of professional self-esteem. The public would continue to demand improving standards from public services: health and education being good examples. Any presumption that new developments require extra money must be broken so that existing expenditure limits could be seen more as firm limits.

One possibility was to strengthen the machinery for scrutinising the effectiveness of existing spending in various areas. For example:

-       could greater flexibility in health care provision enable private funds to be introduced into the NHS?

-       in social security provision, where should the safety net lie? Has it been tested recently?

-       there is a long history of contracting for major defence projects at a price which looked reasonable, but the final bill has often proved much higher;

-       given that changes in expenditure in Scotland are determined by formula, is the time ripe for a review of how far the formula reflects current needs?

Another area where a review of existing expenditure allocations seem desirable is sponsorship for industry. The Departments of Trade & Industry, Employment, Energy and Environment all make provision for various industries. Can we be sure that these do not overlap and that their efforts generate new activity?

Without creating a bureaucracy of performance review, it should be possible for ministers and permanent secretaries to consider 'milestones' for policies: what would be accomplished, by when, and at what cost? The object would be to increase awareness of how much expenditure was being devoted to particular policies within programmes, and to focus attention on the timescale for the achievement of objectives and on the assessment of success or otherwise. By sharpening up the regular evaluation of key policies, permanent secretaries could identify for the benefit of ministers where the government is making significant progress and where policies were being less successful. This would enable options for change to be considered in good time, before the pressures either to reduce spending or to reconsider priorities became acute. More attention might be focused on consumer satisfaction with government services.

The idea of milestones would be particularly useful in simplifying the evaluation of policies. It is important that there should be no centralising effect, either through the re-creation of a Programme Analysis and Review machinery or through the resurrection of a body such as the Central Policy Review Staff. Central inspection sets up the wrong attitudes in line management. The latter are best placed to take a tough view on what is really being achieved and to bring about appropriate changes either to improve performance or to cut losses. External threats are unlikely to have the same effect. Permanent secretaries should be able to do their own reviews, relying on modern management information systems in order to give a picture of performance that could be regularly updated. It is important to ensure that departments have the capacity and the willingness to assess policy self-critically, rather than to provide a central capability through the Cabinet Office or Treasury.

There have been certain reviews where the conclusions had been too sensitive to publish: for example, on the Family Practitioner Services, NHS funding, and social security safety nets. Perhaps that does not matter so long as a firm expectation was established that analysis must lead to action. Too often, reviews are seen as sufficient in themselves, whereas what matters are the actions which result. It has to be recognised that politicians are wary of setting themselves targets because those targets run the risk of becoming hostages to fortune. Another problem is that, particularly with defence spending, the United Kingdom is locked into international projects over which it exerts no direct control over costs.

Removing locally-financed expenditure from the PESC process: *George Jones*

Local government expenditure, to the extent it is financed by local taxes, should be excluded from the public expenditure totals which are determined by the Cabinet in the PESC process. Thus central government should concentrate on the control of its grant to local authorities and on local government borrowing. There are overwhelming economic, fiscal and political arguments for this change. Such expenditure has no effect on the PSBR or on the money supply: it could possibly have an effect on demand if extra local government spending led to lower savings rather than reductions in private expenditure, but the effect would be miniscule, as it would be on interest rates. Although the Treasury wants to control all taxation, other countries allow decentralised governments to draw on a wide range of local taxes without economic mishaps. Central government might have an interest in, or be concerned about, such local spending but it need not directly control it.

Including such spending in the PESC process created an illusion that the centre was in control, and should be in control, of this expenditure. When, as always happened, it did not conform to central targets, the centre felt affronted and sought to control local authorities more tightly. There was a ratchet effect of centralisation. Central government assumed responsibility for what it could not control, and would be blamed for any failure, while local authorities were themselves able to disclaim responsibility because of central intervention. Confrontation between central government and local authorities thus intensified. The latter rightly claimed that the centre demanded more harsh cuts from their services than from its own, as was vividly illustrated in this exercise by the Home Secretary's attempt to reduce his departmental total to meet the Chancellor's figure through cuts in the police and fire services.

If local accountability is defective, then reforms in the electoral system are required, and local taxation should be reformed to find sources of revenue which bear more directly on voters than rates. It is a myth that there are extensive national standards of service promoted by central government. Common standards, emerging from professional and political pressures, would still exist, as now, even if local spending were not in the PESC process. Grant would still be needed, but to do one job only: namely, to equalise for disparities in resources (i.e. taxable capacity, whose best measure is average income per head, since taxes are paid from income).

The Treasury, with its centralising imperialist ambitions, is trying to subvert the Constitution. Its interpretation of the United Kingdom being a unitary state is that the will of government (i.e. the Executive) should be sovereign and should prevail - the assertion of the Stuart kings of the seventeenth century. Under our Constitution, Parliament is sovereign. It had by statute conferred upon local authorities wide policy-making powers: they were not just implementers of central policy. It had by statute given local authorities power to determine their own expenditure and, as a necessary corollary, power to set their own tax rate until the *Rates Act 1984*. Parliament had made them accountable for these policy, spending and taxing decisions, not to Parliament itself, either in the chamber or select committee; nor to central government; but to their own voters. Parliament had singled out local government as a distinctive part of the Constitution by giving it taxation powers and its basis in a local electorate. However, the Treasury saw local government as just an extension of central government, and an inferior part of it.

Select committees and public expenditure planning: *Andrew Likierman*

The timing of decisions on priorities for public expenditure is a crucial factor. Under the present arrangements, priorities are settled either a long way in advance of expenditure allocations and remain protected during much of the PESC process *or* they are settled very late by the Star Chamber on the basis of hard political bargaining and relatively little additional information. There is an argument, therefore, for reviewing how the exercise of defining priorities is carried out. While the principles of the present process should remain, the period from May to July (24 to 21 months before the start of the financial year in question) should be used to obtain input priorities from departmental select committees. This process could be part of the consideration of Estimates for the current year. Such a procedure would give time for ministers to settle priorities in the period October to December, before the new PESC round started. It would give encouragement to select committees in that they would know that their findings could be an input to ministerial decision-making.

Against such a proposal, it is likely to be argued that the membership of select committees makes them unequal to the task of considering Estimates, and the committees have a tendency to operate in a partisan way. Similarly, it is said that they are fond of discussing the operation of current policies, and are less interested in priorities, even less in the audit function. Nevertheless, one advantage of this proposal is that it would become more difficult for ministers to reverse their view on priorities within a short time of having established it. Moreover, PESC ought to function as a process of continuous evaluation and review so that it becomes more realistic and depends less on the intervention of the Star Chamber to settle expenditure figures and thus determine important priorities.

7.   The Bid Book

Introduction

This simulation exercise on 'Altering Public Expenditure at the Margin' is just that - a simulation. As such, it provides a means of exploring, through group discussion and negotiation, the problems of increasing *or* decreasing public expenditure by British central government today.

The advantage of simulation is that a variety of different ways can be run through in order to see whether, or to what extent, ways of organising collective decision-making alter outcomes in public expenditure. Spending decisions sometimes involve differences of opinion about increases, at other times cuts, and often a combination of increases and cuts. It is important to test methods of decision-making under different alternatives.

The bids in this Bid Book have been prepared by experts in specific areas of public policy paralleling government departments. They are not intended to represent the views of any particular party, separately or collectively. Many views about what government should do are affected by expertise, and by the bi-partisan proclivity of ministers responsible for spending to want to spend more.

In order to avoid strict mimicking of the position of the government of the day, the bids have been prepared with an illustrative assumption that public expenditure might rise to a higher level than currently published figures. In practice, the bids contain dozens of proposals to cut spending on particular programmes, as well as dozens of proposals to increase spending. The Bid Book can therefore be used in exercises simulating cuts in public expenditure, as well as increases.

A small point should be made about programme numbering. In the Bid Book, we have simply numbered sequentially the programmes for which the simulation weekend had ministers.   However, there is frequent reference in the departmental texts and tables to the sub-programme numbers of the 1986 public expenditure White Paper (Cmnd 9702, Treasury 1986a).

In the preparation of this Bid Book, many people played a significant part, especially the individual departmental 'ministers' and the 'Cabinet Office team'. In editing, typing and checking the figures contained herein, Dr. Phillip Davies, Ms Anne Shaw and Ms Isobel Rogerson of the Centre for the Study of Public Policy, University of Strathclyde, and Ms Lynn Starr of the Public Finance Foundation provided essential services.

Professor Richard Rose, Co-ordinator

October, 1986

TABLE 7A SIMULATION BIDS COMPARED TO TREASURY PROPOSALS, 1986/87 - 1989/90

| | TREASURY | | OUR NEXT YEAR'S BIDS | | | OUR BIDS FOR 1989/90 | | |
	1 Cmnd 9702 1986/87	2 Cmnd 9702 1987/88	3 1987/88	4 Up from 1986/87	5 Up from 1987/88	6 1989/90	7 Up from 1986/87	8 Up from 1987/88
	£m	£m	£m	£m	£m	£m	£m	£m
DHSS (1)	60,656	62,850	65,534	4,878	2,684	71,964	11,308	9,114
Employment	3,741	3,790	5,950	2,209	2,160	10,192	6,451	6,402
Defence	18,525	18,820	19,820	1,295	1,000	22,375	3,850	3,555
Education & Science (2)	14,319	14,400	15,479	1,160	1,079	17,424	3,105	3,024
Scotland	7,573	7,410	7,561	(12)	151	8,359	786	949
Environment	6,374	6,360	6,965	591	605	7,280	906	920
Trade & Industry	1,581	1,260	1,819	238	559	2,009	428	749
Home Office	5,531	5,531	6,150	619	619	6,476	945	945
Transport	4,809	4,840	5,238	429	398	5,551	742	711
Agriculture	2,170	2,250	2,658	488	408	2,702	532	452
Energy	115	(550)	(280)	(395)	270	(300)	(415)	250
FCO	1,959	2,010	2,079	120	69	2,204	245	194
Other Depts (3)	12,342	13,429	14,436	2,094	1,007	16,249	3,907	2,820
Contingency Reserve	4,500	6,250	6,250	1,750	0	9,750	5,250	3,500
Privatisation net	(4,750)	(4,750)	(4,750)	0	0	0	4,750	4,750
TOTAL BIDS	139,445	143,900	154,909	15,464	11,009	182,235	42,790	38,335
Simulation allows				9,455	5,000		19,455	15,000
Amount to be cut				6,009	6,009		23,335	23,335
(1) Of which :								
Social Security	42,932	44,400	45,840	2,908	1,440	49,900	6,698	5,500
Health & PSS	17,724	18,450	19,219	1,495	769	21,584	3,860	3,134

(2) Education estimated to increase in the same proportion as other departments: 7.5% for 1986/87, and 21% for 1989/90.

(3) European Community, Arts and Libraries, Wales, NIO, Chancellor's Departments grossed up 7.5 % for 1986/87, and 21 % for 1989/90.

Source : Cmnd 9702, Table 2.1, *Planning total by department*. With the exception of the Home Office, column 1 figures come directly from Cmnd 9702; on that, there is an accidental difference of minus £18m. Because the simulation computer did its own rounding, there are minor differences. Column 1 above ignored the adjustment line (re. nationalised industries to be privatised) in Cmnd 9702 and this accounts for the difference from the White Paper 1986/87 planning total.

TABLE 7B: CONSOLIDATED LIST OF PROPOSED SPENDING CHANGES

A. PROPOSED CASH INCREASES, 1989/90 OVER 1986/87

£m

DHSS:Social Security	7,268
EMP:4.7 Promotion & preservation of emp. opportunities etc.	5,404
DHSS:11.1 Hospital & Community Health - Current exp. gross	2,804
MoD:Air Force general purpose forces	1,113
DoE:Housing-Gross capital expenditure	1,097
MoD:Navy general purpose combat forces	1,000
DHSS:11.1 Family Practitioner Services - Current exp. gross	961
MoD:European theatre ground forces	936
EMP:4.7 General labour market services	726
MoD:Nuclear strategic forces	542
DoE:Environmental services-excl. Urban Prog. Current. exp.	485
MAFF:Market support/IBAP	467
MoD:Research and development	423
EMP:4.7 Manpower Services Commission	420
HO:Penal system - Local Authority - Current	349
SCOT:Education	308
SCOT:Health & Personal Social Services	297
HO:Court Services - Criminal Injuries Comp. Board	269
HO:Court Services - Receipts	260
DoT:LA:6.2 Roads maintenance	242
ENGY:Public corporations: 4.13 Other	216
DoT:LA: Capital - Roads	208
DoT:6.1 National roads systems - New construction	185
DHSS:Personal Social Services:Current spending - gross	176
DTI:Regional and general industrial support	166
SCOT:Housing	155
DoE:Housing-Capital receipts	151
FCO:2.5 ODA:Net aid programme	149
HO:9.7 Community services	145
DoE:Environmental services-excl. Urban Prog. Cap. exp.	130
SCOT:Roads & Transport	113
DHSS:11.3 Central Health & Misc. Services-Current exp.- gross	110
DoT:Initiatives - London deregulation grant	100
MoD:Reserve/Auxiliary formations	92
SCOT:Other environmental services	92
DoT:6.1 National roads systems - Structural maintenance	75
MAFF:Structural measures/MAFF	75
DTI:Support for industry	74

TABLE 7B: CONSOLIDATED LIST OF PROPOSED SPENDING CHANGES

A.   PROPOSED CASH INCREASES, 1989/90 OVER 1986/87 (Cont.)

£m

HO:Penal system - Local Authority - Capital	64
HO:Penal system - Central government	56
ENGY:4.2 Research and development: Non nuclear	55
DHSS:11.1 Hospital & Community Health - Capital expenditure	55
HO:Fire Service - Local Authority - Current	53
SCOT:Law, order & protective services	50
MoD:War and contingency stocks	45
DTI:ECGD - Interest support costs	43
MoD:Training	43
DTI:International trade	42
DoE:8.9 Public corporations - New Towns	42
DoT:Initiatives - Non-rural, non-Met bus grant	40
ENGY:4.2 R&D: Nuclear	39
HO:Fire Service - Local Authority - Capital	39
FCO:2.1 Overseas representation	37
DTI:Regional and general industrial support	35
HO:Immigration - Immigration control	34
FCO:2.2 Other external relations	34
DoT:Initiatives - Tolled crossings	32
HO:Court services - Central government	31
HO:Fire service - Central government	29
DoE: 7.6 Current exp. - Local authority administration	28
MAFF:Market support/MAFF	25
DTI:Support for aerospace, shipbldg., steel and vehicle manufacture	22
DoT:Initiatives - London traffic enforcement agency	21
DoT:Initiatives - Accident Investigation & Prev. Grant	21
DoE:Environmental services - Local Authority rate collection	21
HO:Court services - Local Authority - Current	21
DoT:6.1 National roads systems - Current maintenance	20
DoT:6.3 Bus grants	20
MAFF:Forestry Commission	17
DoE:8.4 Environmental services - Historic buildings	16
FCO:2.3 External broadcasting	13
DoT:Public corporations: National Bus Company	13
SCOT:Agriculture, fisheries, food	13

TABLE 7B: CONSOLIDATED LIST OF PROPOSED SPENDING CHANGES

A. PROPOSED CASH INCREASES, 1989/90 OVER 1986/87 (Cont.)

£m

DoT:LA: Capital - Trading services	12
FCO:2.4 British Council	12
DoT:6.8 Driver & vehicle licensing	12
HO:Immigration - Passport Office	10
DoT:6.7 Roads & transport admin.	10
DTI:Public corporations - Nat. inds'. EFLs Voted in Estimates	10
DTI:ECGD - Cost escalation guarantees	9
DHSS:Personal Social Services:GP Finance Corporation	8
DoT:6.3 BR pensions & other	8
EMP:4.8 Central services	8
SCOT:Other public services	8
SCOT:Arts and libraries	8
DTI:Central and miscellaneous services	8
DoE:8.3 Environmental services - Royal palaces and parks	7
DHSS:11.1 Family Practitioner Services - Capital expenditure	7
ENGY:4.8 Other central and misc. services	7
DTI:Public corporations - Other	6
DTI:LA-Relvt.cur.exp-Regulation of domestic tr,ind, cons.prot.	6
EMP:4.9 Health & Safety Commission	6
DTI:ECGD - Mixed credit matching facility	6
MAFF: Animal health/MAFF	5
DHSS:11.3 Central Health & Misc. Services-Capital expenditure	5
EMP:4.7 Advisory Conciliation and Arb. Service	5
DoT:6.7 Research and development	5
DoE:8.6 Environmental services - Grants to environmental bodies	5
FCO:2.6 ODA:Overseas aid administration	4
ENGY:4.1 Other support services	4
DoT:6.3 Freight facilities grants	4
ENGY:4.2 Promotion of energy efficiency	4
FCO:2.7 ODA:Other external relations	4
EMP:4.7 LA:Relevant current exp. - Careers service	3
DoT:6.7 Licensing & testing	3
EMP:4.7 Services for seriously disabled people	3
DoE:8.1 Environmental services - Water research and services	3
MAFF:Administration/IBAP	3
DoT:6.7 Road safety	3
DoE:Environmental services - Records & Reg. of vital stats.	3
EMP:4.7 LA:Rel.cur.exp. - Services for seriously disabled	3

TABLE 7B: CONSOLIDATED LIST OF PROPOSED SPENDING CHANGES

A. PROPOSED CASH INCREASES, 1989/90 OVER 1986/87 (Cont.)

£m

MAFF:Fishery support/MAFF	2
DoT:6.3 NFC pensions	2
DTI:Regulation of domestic trade, industry, consumer protection	2
DoT:6.4 Shipping services	2
DoE:7.6 Current exp. - Housing associations	2
MAFF:Projects assisted by EC/MAFF	2
ENGY:Other central govt. 4.2 research and development:Nuclear	2
SCOT:Tourism	2
MAFF:Civil defence/MAFF	1
SCOT:Local Authority unallocated current expenditure	1
DoT:6.4 Ports	1

122 Proposed Increases   29,208

B. PROPOSED CASH DECREASES, 1989/90 OVER 1986/87

£m

EMP:4.7 Careers service grant	(1)
DHSS:11.3 Central Health & Misc. Services - Current exp-charges	(1)
MAFF:Other services/MAFF	(1)
DoT:6.7 International subs etc.	(1)
DHSS:Personal Social Services:Current spending - charges	(1)
DoT:9.4 Civil defence	(2)
MAFF:National market support/MAFF	(2)
HO:Civil Defence - Local Authority - Capital	(2)
HO:Police - Local Authority - Current	(3)
EMP:4.7 LA:Non-relevant current exp. Careers Service	(3)
EMP:4.1 Small firms etc. support services	(3)
DoT:6.9 Other public corporations	(4)
EMP:Public corporations - National Dock Labour Board	(4)
EMP:4.7 LA:Capital - Services for seriously disabled	(5)
MoD:Miscellaneous items	(5)
ENGY:4.1 Selective assistance to firms & undertakings	(6)
HO:Court Services - Legal Aid	(7)
DoT:6.6 Civil aviation services	(8)
HO:9.8 Miscellaneous and central services	(8)
FCO:2.9 ODA:Public corporations	(8)

TABLE 7B: CONSOLIDATED LIST OF PROPOSED SPENDING CHANGES

B. PROPOSED CASH DECREASES, 1989/90 OVER 1986/87 (Cont.)

£m

HO:Police - Local Authority - Capital	(12)
DoT:Public corporations:Civil Aviation Authority	(14)
DHSS:11.1 Hospital & Community Health - Current exp. - charges	(14)
DoE:8.6 Environmental services - Departmental administration	(15)
HO:Civil Defence - Local Authority - Current	(15)
DoT:Public corporations:6.5 British Airports Authority	(15)
DoT:6.4 Ports	(17)
HO:Police - Government	(18)
ENGY:4.14 Other pub. corps. Voted in Estimates - UKAEA	(19)
SCOT:Industry, energy, trade & employment	(22)
DoE:8.5 Environmental services - Regional & industrial support	(27)
MAFF:Arterial drainage/MAFF	(28)
DoE:8.9 Public corporations - UDCs	(30)
MAFF:Research, advice, admin./MAFF	(34)
DoT:LA:Revenue support & concessionary fares	(47)
HO:Civil defence - Central government	(48)
MoD:Other Army combat forces	(49)
DHSS:11.1 Family Practitioner Services - Current exp. - charges	(68)
DoT:Public corporations: British Railways Board	(71)
HO:Court services - Courts	(73)
DoE:8.2 Environmental services - Derelict land reclamation	(78)
HO:Court services - Local Authority - Capital	(79)
MoD:Equipment support/facilities	(108)
DoE:8.1 Nat. inds'. EFLs	(108)
EMP:4.7 Redundancy & Maternity Pay Funds	(113)
DoT:Public corporations: London Regional Transport	(121)
HO:Penal System - Prisons	(150)
MoD:Other support	(184)
ENGY:4.4 Redundant mineworkers' payments scheme	(186)
DoE:8.8 Environmental services - Urban Programme	(227)
SCOT:Nationalised industries	(239)
ENGY:Public corporations:4.13 Nat. inds'. EFLs Voted in Estimates	(530)
DoE:7.1 Current exp. - Subsidies for revenue deficits	(600)

53 Proposed Decreases (3,434)

TABLE 7B: CONSOLIDATED LIST OF PROPOSED SPENDING CHANGES

C.   NO CASH CHANGE, 1989/90 OVER 1986/87

£m

DTI:OtherPub. corps. - English Industrial Estates Corporation	0
EMP:4.1 Promotion of tourism	0
DTI:LA-Cap. exp. - regulation of domestic tr, ind, consumer protec.	0
DHSS:Personal Social Services:Capital expenditure	0
DoT:LA:Other	0
DoE:8.6 Environmental services - Environmental research	0

6 No Proposed Changes $\overline{0}$

Note: Combining the increases and decreases in Table 7B does not produce the net expenditure change for 1989/90 given in Table 7A.   No lines can be entered for departments where only an aggregate total was provided.

7.1 Ministry of Defence

David Greenwood

1.   The Ministry of Defence welcomes the Chancellor's intimation that he is prepared to see the planning total for public expenditure rise to £148.9bn for 1987/88, £153.7bn for 1988/89 and £158.2bn for 1989/90.

2.   The implication is that, along with other Departments, we need no longer consider ourselves bound by the tight cash limits for 1987/88 and 1988/89 (and, implicitly, for 1989/90) which emerged from the 1985 Public Expenditure Survey 'round' and were published in Cmnd 9702.

3.   Relaxation of these stringent limits will ease the problems of managing the defence programme. Staying within the straitjacket of the Cmnd 9702 figures would have necessitated significant - and, in some instances, politically damaging - adjustments in the scope and scale of the defence effort. In the *Statement of the Defence Estimates 1986* (Cmnd 9763, Ministry of Defence 1986) this was acknowledged, obliquely, in the references to the 'difficult decisions' required to bring the defence programme into line with the cash to be made available. However, the media, the political community generally and the House of Commons' Defence Committee (1986) particularly recognised our White Paper language for the weasel wording that it was; and some of the resultant speculation regarding the kind of programme adjustments which would be necessary has been uncomfortably close to the mark.

4.   In drawing up revised defence budget targets covering 1987/88-1989/90 for this first stage of the 1986 expenditure planning 'round' we have, therefore, chosen to use our new (limited) freedom of manoeuvre not for new departures but to preserve elements of the forward programme which were seriously at risk. On the new bid for 1987/88 and proposed target Estimates for 1988/89 and 1989/90 we will be able to:

-    sustain the momentum of the Trident acquisition, which has been *the* overriding priority in our programme since 1980 (and for which we were contemplating a modest slowdown);

-    order further Type 23 frigates and Upholder-class submarines at a rate sufficiently close to that to which we committed ourselves in 1983/84 - 3 per year/1 per year respectively - so as to deflect criticism that we have abandoned that aim (as we would undoubtedly have had to do in the absence of the extra budgetary headroom now available);

-       order an additional Challenger tank regiment and put aside the set of contingency plans which had been prepared for stretching the procurement timetable for certain other Army equipment programmes;

-       confirm an 'attrition buy' of Tornado aircraft, further conversion of VC-10s to the tanker role and our firm participation in both the European Fighter Aircraft and NATO helicopter programmes - all of which have been on 'hold' while we have been considering how best to accommodate to the tightly-drawn cash limits of Cmnd 9702; and

-       increase purchases of ammunition for stock replenishment - for which, incidentally, Royal Ordnance plc has been pressing - and of a variety of other stores and spares (enabling us to meet the 'sustainability' goals to which our NATO allies attach importance but which we had, of necessity, relegated to a very low priority in the programme).

On any allocation of resources *less* than that proposed - see Tables 7.1A and 7.1B - one or more of these rehabilitations of the defence effort will have to be foregone.

5.   In considering how much of the newly-available budgetary headroom the MoD should lay claim to we have been influenced by two factors:

(a)   the existence of powerful domestic political imperatives for additional social expenditures in the short term; and

(b)   the insistent pressure from our NATO allies - and especially from the United States - for, if not enhancement of our contribution to the Alliance's conventional defences, at least no diminution or dilution of that contribution during the later 1980s.

Because of (a) there is clearly no case for a disproportionate allocation of 'new money' to Defence in 1987/88. Because of (b), however, it would be unwise to present new public expenditure plans in which the MoD is not accorded something like its fair share of extra funds in the forthcoming financial year; and it is desirable that we should, in later years, come back into line with respect to NATO Resource Guidance - which means budgeting for 3% real increases in annual expenditures (as we did from 1979 to 1984).

6.   Hence, the revised spending bid for 1987/88 (Table 7.1A) provides for a 6.99% cash increase over 1986/87, equal to the overall year-on-year percentage increase in the cash planning total (revised). The amended spending profile for 1988/89 and 1989/90 (Table 7.1B) provides for subsequent cash increases of 6.51% and 5.99%, these being the amounts necessary to yield 3% growth year-on-year (given the expected inflation rate). The detail in both Tables indicates that extra funds will be applied to almost all aspects of defence mission programmes. Very little will be applied to support programmes where we expect to hold our own, thanks to the efficiency programme described in Cmnd 9763.

7.   The justification for the cash increase for 1987/88 over 1986/87 is, as stated, to permit us to sustain the existing balanced defence effort and proceed with necessary equipment modernisation in accordance with existing policy. No specific claim is made to take account of the Relative Price Effect which, recent evidence suggests, may be approaching zero with the continuing positive component attributable to pay factors offset by a negative component attributable to non-pay items (the effect of falling fuel costs and the effect of our competition policy in defence procurement).

8.   We invite endorsement of a Defence Estimate of £19,820m for 1987/88 (compared with the £18,820m of Cmnd 9702). We invite endorsement of Target Estimates for 1988/89 of £21,110m and for 1989/90 of £22,375m. These amounts represent, respectively, 13.3%, 13.7% and 14.1% of the Chancellor's revised planning totals.

TABLE 7.1A   MINISTRY OF DEFENCE

	1986/87 Expend. (Cmnd 9702)	1987/88 Revised Plan	Absolute Change 1987/88-1986/87	Percent Change 1987/88-1986/87
	£m	£m	£m	%
Mission Programmes				
Nuclear strategic forces	658	1,000	342	52
Navy general purpose combat forces	2,625	2,900	275	10
European theatre ground forces	2,814	3,025	211	7
Other army combat forces	204	200	(4)	(2)
Air Force general purpose forces	3,687	4,000	313	8
Reserve/auxiliary formations	358	400	42	12
SUB-TOTAL	10,346	11,525	1,179	11
Support Programmes				
Research and development	2,327	2,450	123	5
Training	1,257	1,300	43	3
Equipment support/facilities	983	975	(8)	(1)
War and contingency stocks	405	450	45	11
Other support	3,184	3,100	(84)	(3)
Miscellaneous items	25	20	(5)	(20)
SUB-TOTAL	8,181	8,295	114	1
TOTAL - MoD (Net)	18,527	19,820	1,293	7

TABLE 7.1B   MINISTRY OF DEFENCE

	1986/87 Expenditure (Cmnd 9702) £m	1986/87 Estimated Outturn £m	1987/88 Revised Plan £m	1988/89 Revised Plan £m	1989/90 Plan £m	Absolute Change 1989/90-1986/87 £m	Percentage Change 1989/90-1986/87 %
Mission Programmes							
Nuclear strategic forces	658	634	1,000	1,100	1,200	542	82
Navy general purpose combat forces	2,625	2,575	2,900	3,275	3,625	1,000	38
European theatre ground forces	2,814	2,830	3,025	3,400	3,750	936	33
Other army combat forces	204	210	200	175	155	(49)	(24)
Air Force general purpose forces	3,687	3,785	4,000	4,430	4,800	1,113	30
Reserve/auxiliary formations	358	363	400	435	450	92	26
SUB-TOTAL	10,346	10,397	11,525	12,815	13,980	3,634	35
Support Programmes							
Research and development	2,327	2,381	2,450	2,600	2,750	423	18
Training	1,257	1,266	1,300	1,300	1,300	43	3
Equipment support/facilities	983	1,033	975	925	875	(108)	(11)
War and contingency stocks	405	400	450	450	450	45	11
Other support	3,184	3,200	3,100	3,000	3,000	(184)	(6)
Miscellaneous items	25	25	20	20	20	(5)	(20)
SUB-TOTAL	8,181	8,305	8,295	8,295	8,395	214	3
TOTAL - MoD (Net)	18,527	18,702	19,820	21,110	22,375	3,848	21

7.2 Foreign & Commonwealth Office

William Wallace

The numbered points below relate to the equivalent lines in Tables 7.2A and 7.2B.

1.   Additional funding is sought for 1987/88, above the £400m originally planned, to cover:

(a)   £10m as the first instalment of a crash programme of £20m over two years to improve physical security at British posts overseas against the threat of terrorist attack; and

(b)   £4m to provide some flexibility in the staffing and management of overseas posts, after a period of sustained cuts and increasing demands, and to compensate for the overseas price effect and for adverse exchange rate movements.

It is anticipated that some savings will be made in the 1989/90 financial year through moves towards collocation and shared services with other EC governments for overseas posts in a number of third countries.

2.   Expenditure under programme 2.2 is 'distorted' by a number of special payments and reimbursements. The 1986/87 figures as shown are thus 16.2% lower than the total estimate provisions and forecast outturn for 1985/86, and some 7.4% lower than actual expenditure for 1985/86 due to the inclusion of £19m repayment of principal on a special loan to Yugoslavia. A further £4m is credited against programme 2.2 in 1986/87 for interest payments on the outstanding balances, as against £6m for the two preceding years. The 'base' figure for 1986/87, without this, becomes £111m, comparable to the £110m shown for 1985/86. The completion of repayment accounts for the apparent sharp increase in the 1988/89 financial year.

3.   No increases are requested under this heading beyond those previously set out in Cmnd 9702.

4.   An additional £3m is included in addition to the £50m originally planned, to restore to the British Council a further year of stable funding in real terms beyond the three years agreed with the Treasury in

1983/84. £8m is also allocated, for a period of five years, for the proposed 'Thatcher Package', to be announced at the London European Council in December 1986, for a major expansion of the European exchanges programme, concentrating in particular on exchanges of experts in science, technology and engineering, and on youth exchanges linked to training programmes and to work experience. HM Government will be proposing to its European partner governments that the bulk of funds available under the package should be dependent upon matching funds being made available either by other governments or by the private sector.

5.   An additional £41m is requested, above the £1,230m originally planned, to cover:

(a)   £25m for medium-term support for countries affected by the recent drought in sub-Saharan Africa, including budgetary and balance-of-payments support to assist governments in adjusting domestic economic policies in the light of IMF recommendations, and support for voluntary agencies in agricultural development and reafforestations schemes;

(b)   £5m to restore the cuts necessitated in the ODA contributions to the British Council (BC) by unanticipated demands for expenditure on famine relief in Africa, and to enable the BC to expand its work in technical and vocational training in countries affected by drought;

(c)   £10m to assist states in Southern Africa adversely affected by the deteriorating situation in South Africa and by the impact of international sanctions and internal disruptions on the South African economy; and

(d)   £1m to establish a scholarship scheme to enable a small number of black South Africans whose education has been disrupted to continue their studies in Britain.

6.   This represents no change in the totals previously planned.

7.   This programme primarily covers pension supplements and other pension-related payments for some 36,000 past employees of former UK dependencies and their widows.

8.   This programme has covered financial support for the Crown Agents and other similar agencies; such support will no longer be required after the 1986/87 financial year.

TABLE 7.2A   FOREIGN & COMMONWEALTH OFFICE

	1986/87 Expend. (Cmnd 9702)	1987/88 Revised Plan	Absolute Change 1987/88- 1986/87	Percent Change 1987/88- 1986/87
	£m	£m	£m	%
FCO-Diplomatic, Information, Culture				
2.1 Overseas representation	387	414	27	7
2.2 Other external relations	92	93	1	1
2.3 External broadcasting & monitoring	111	120	9	8
2.4 British Council	51	61	10	20
TOTAL - FCO-Diplomatic, Information, Culture	641	688	47	7
FCO-Overseas Development Administration				
2.5 Net aid programme	1,187	1,271	84	7
2.6 Overseas aid administration	27	30	3	11
2.7 Other external relations	96	90	(6)	(6)
2.9 Public corporations	8			
TOTAL - FCO-ODA	1,318	1,391	73	6
TOTAL FOREIGN & COMMONWEALTH OFFICE	1,959	2,079	120	6

TABLE 7.2B   FOREIGN & COMMONWEALTH OFFICE

	1986/87 Expenditure (Cmnd 9702) £m	1986/87 Estimated Outturn £m	1987/88 Revised Plan £m	1988/89 Revised Plan £m	1989/90 Plan £m	Absolute Change 1989/90-1986/87 £m	Percentage Change 1989/90-1986/87 %
FCO-Diplomatic, Information, Culture							
2.1 Overseas representation	387	389	414	424	424	37	10
2.2 Other external relations	92	94	93	123	126	34	37
2.3 External broadcasting & monitoring	111	111	120	120	124	13	12
2.4 British Council	51	51	61	61	63	12	24
TOTAL - FCO-Dip.,Info.,Culture	641	645	688	728	737	96	15
FCO - Overseas Development Administration							
2.5 Net aid programme	1,187	1,177	1,271	1,311	1,336	149	13
2.6 Overseas aid administration	27	27	30	30	31	4	15
2.7 Other external relations	96	95	90	100	100	4	4
2.9 Public corporations	8	8					
TOTAL - FCO-ODA.	1,318	1,307	1,391	1,441	1,467	149	11
TOTAL - FOREIGN & COMMONWEALTH OFFICE	1,959	1,952	2,079	2,169	2,204	245	13

7.3 Ministry of Agriculture, Fisheries & Food

Allan Buckwell

1.   Of total expenditure by this Ministry, over 70% is spent through the Common Agricultural Policy. The majority of this in turn is for market support through the activities of the Intervention Board for Agricultural Produce. This is mostly obligatory expenditure whose volume depends to a very great extent on the size of the harvest (principally of cereals, dairy produce, beef and sheepmeat), its quality and prices agreed by the Council of Agricultural Ministers together with prices in world markets.

2.   The large increases shown for 1987/88 incorporate the serious understatement of 1986/87 plus allowances for productivity increases in oilseeds, beef and sheepmeat production. It is assumed that there will continue to be price cuts in cereals which neutralise the additional output of cereals, and that production growth in dairy products has been arrested by production quotas.

3.   Thus, the estimates from 1987/88 to 1989/90 show a more modest rate of increase indicating the success of the restraint in agricultural prices and the production effect of this policy. As is always the case with these estimates there is a wide margin of error due to production conditions outside the control of the Ministry.

4.   With the exception of structural measures and expenditures on animal health, spending under national control shows a much smaller increase and in many programmes a cut. The biggest such cut is in the advisory services.

5.   Structural spending is projected to rise. This is a direct consequence of the cut in real price supports. The increased structural spending is necessary to shield those farmers most hurt by price cuts, and more positively to assist farmers to adjust to the new market realities.

6.   No estimates of the receipts from the European Agricultural Guidance and Guarantee Fund are made.

TABLE 7.3A   MINISTRY OF AGRICULTURE, FISHERIES & FOOD

		1986/87 Expend. (Cmnd 9702)	1987/88 Revised Plan	Absolute Change 1987/88- 1986/87	Percent Change 1987/88- 1986/87
		£m	£m	£m	%
European Community					
Market support	IBAP	1,383	1,816	433	31
	MAFF	61	85	24	39
Projects assisted by EC	MAFF	10	11	1	10
Administration	IBAP	27	30	3	11
Total IBAP and other CAP	IBAP	1,410	1,846	436	31
	MAFF	71	96	25	35
SUB-TOTAL		1,481	1,942	461	31
Domestic					
National market support	MAFF	12	10	(2)	(17)
Structural measures	MAFF	119	166	47	39
Animal health	MAFF	15	20	5	33
Other services	MAFF	91	90	(1)	(1)
Fishery support	MAFF	28	30	2	7
Arterial drainage	MAFF	148	140	(8)	(5)
Research, advice, admin.	MAFF	214	200	(14)	(7)
Civil defence	MAFF	9	10	1	11
SUB-TOTAL		636	666	30	5
SUB-TOTAL: Forestry Commission		53	50	(3)	(6)
TOTAL		2,170	2,658	488	22
Analysis:	IBAP	1,410	1,846	436	31
	MAFF	707	762	55	8
	Forestry Com.	53	50	(3)	(6)

Abbreviations used in Tables:

IBAP = Intervention Board for Agricultural Produce
MAFF = Ministry of Agriculture, Fisheries & Food

TABLE 7.3B MINISTRY OF AGRICULTURE, FISHERIES & FOOD

		1986/87 Expenditure (Cmnd 9702) £m	1986/87 Estimated Outturn £m	1987/88 Revised Plan £m	1988/89 Revised Plan £m	1989/90 Plan £m	Absolute Change 1989/90-1986/87 £m	Percentage Change 1989/90-1986/87 %
European Community								
Market support	IBAP	1,383	1,700	1,816	1,856	1,850	467	34
	MAFF	61	84	85	87	86	25	41
Projects assisted by EC	MAFF	10	9	11	11	12	2	20
Administration	IBAP	27	22	30	30	30	3	11
Total IBAP and other CAP	IBAP	1,410	1,722	1,846	1,886	1,880	470	33
	MAFF	71	93	96	98	98	27	38
SUB-TOTAL		1,481	1,815	1,942	1,984	1,978	497	34
Domestic								
National market support	MAFF	12	15	10	10	10	(2)	(17)
Structural measures	MAFF	119	157	166	176	194	75	63
Animal health	MAFF	15	15	20	20	20	5	33
Other services	MAFF	91	95	90	90	90	(1)	(1)
Fishery support	MAFF	28	31	30	30	30	2	7
Arterial drainage	MAFF	148	171	140	130	120	(28)	(19)
Research, advice, admin.	MAFF	214	210	200	200	180	(34)	(16)
Civil defence	MAFF	9	9	10	10	10	1	11
SUB-TOTAL		636	703	666	666	654	18	3
SUB-TOTAL: Forestry Commission		53	53	50	60	70	17	32
TOTAL		2,170	2,571	2,658	2,710	2,702	532	25
Analysis:	IBAP	1,410	1,722	1,846	1,886	1,880	470	33
	MAFF	707	796	762	764	752	45	6
	Forestry Com.	53	53	50	60	70	17	32

7.4 Department of Trade & Industry

Daniel Jeffreys

No text was supplied.

TABLE 7.4A   DEPARTMENT OF TRADE & INDUSTRY

	1986/87 Expend. (Cmnd 9702)	1987/88 Revised Plan	Absolute Change 1987/88- 1986/87	Percent Change 1987/88- 1986/87
	£m	£m	£m	%
CENTRAL GOVERNMENT				
Voted in Estimates				
Regional and general industrial support	374	450	76	20
Support for industry	395	430	35	9
Support for aerospace, shipbuilding, steel and vehicle manufacture	181	188	7	4
International trade	42	84	42	100
Regulation of domestic trade and industry, and consumer protection	27	28	1	4
Central and miscellaneous services	121	125	4	3
Civil defence				
Total Voted in Estimates	1,140	1,305	165	14
Other central government				
Regional and general industrial support	(35)	(30)	5	(14)
Support for aerospace, shipbuilding, steel and vehicle manufacture	(7)		7	(100)
Total other central government	(42)	(30)	12	(29)
TOTAL - CENTRAL GOVERNMENT	1,098	1,275	177	16
LOCAL AUTHORITIES				
Relevant current spending				
Regulation of domestic trade and industry, and consumer protection	67	69	2	3
Local authority capital				
Regulation of domestic trade and inustry, and consumer protection	2	2	0	0
TOTAL - LOCAL AUTHORITIES	69	71	2	3
PUBLIC CORPORATIONS				
Nationalised industries' EFLs				
Voted in Estimates	73	80	7	10
Other	47	50	3	6
Total nationalised industries' EFLs	120	130	10	8
Other public corporations				
English Industrial Estates Corporation	13	13	0	0
TOTAL - PUBLIC CORPORATIONS	133	143	10	8
TOTAL DTI	1,300	1,489	189	15
EXPORT CREDITS GUARANTEE DEPARTMENT (ECGD)				
Central government				
Cost escalation guarantees	13	20	7	54
Interest support costs	262	300	38	15
Mixed credit matching facility	5	10	5	100
Total voted expenditure	280	330	50	18
TOTAL ECGD	280	330	50	18
TOTAL DTI & ECGD	1,580	1,819	239	15

TABLE 7.4B DEPARTMENT OF TRADE AND INDUSTRY

	1986/87 Expend. (Cmnd 9702) £m	1986/87 Estimated Outturn £m	1987/88 Revised Plan £m	1988/89 Revised Plan £m	1989/90 Plan £m	Absolute Change 1989/90-1986/87 £m	Percent Change 1989/90-1986/87 %
CENTRAL GOVERNMENT							
Voted in Estimates							
Regional and general industrial support	374	374	450	540	540	166	44
Support for industry	395	395	430	469	469	74	19
Support for aerospace, shipbuilding, steel and vehicle manufacture	181	181	188	196	196	15	8
International trade	42	42	84	84	84	42	100
Regulation of domestic trade and industry, and consumer protection	27	27	28	29	29	2	7
Central and miscellaneous services	121	121	125	129	129	8	7
Civil defence							
Total Voted in Estimates	1,140	1,140	1,305	1,447	1,447	307	27
Other central government							
Regional and general industrial support	(35)	(35)	(30)	(30)		35	(100)
Support for aerospace, shipbuilding, steel and vehicle manufacture	(7)	(7)				7	(100)
Total other central government	(42)	(42)	(30)	(30)	0	42	(100)
TOTAL – CENTRAL GOVERNMENT	1,098	1,098	1,275	1,417	1,447	349	32
LOCAL AUTHORITIES							
Relevant current spending							
Regulation of domestic trade and industry, and consumer protection	67	67	69	71	73	6	9
Local authority capital							
Regulation of domestic trade and industry, and consumer protection	2	2	2	2	2	0	0
TOTAL – LOCAL AUTHORITIES	69	69	71	73	75	6	9

Contd........

TABLE 7.4B   DEPARTMENT OF TRADE & INDUSTRY (Continued)

	1986/87 Expend. (Cmnd 9702) £m	1986/87 Estimated Outturn £m	1987/88 Revised Plan £m	1988/89 Revised Plan £m	1989/90 Plan £m	Absolute Change 1989/90-1987/88 £m	Percent Change 1989/90-1987/88 %
PUBLIC CORPORATIONS							
Nationalised industries' EFLs							
Voted in Estimates	73	73	80	82	83	10	14
Other	47	47	50	52	53	6	13
Total nationalised industries' EFLs	120	120	130	134	136	16	13
Other public corporations							
English Industrial Estates Corporation	13	13	13	13	13	0	0
TOTAL – PUBLIC CORPORATIONS	133	133	143	147	149	16	12
TOTAL DTI	1,300	1,300	1,489	1,637	1,671	371	29
EXPORT CREDITS GUARANTEE DEPARTMENT (ECGD)							
Central government							
Cost escalation guarantees	13	13	20	21	22	9	69
Interest support costs	262	262	300	303	305	43	16
Mixed credit matching facility	5	5	10	11	11	6	120
Total voted expenditure	280	280	330	335	338	58	21
TOTAL – ECGD	280	280	330	335	338	58	21
TOTAL – DTI & ECGD	1,580	1,580	1,819	1,972	2,009	429	27

7.5 Department of Energy

Graham Hadley

1.   At this stage, changes shown in Tables 7.5A and 7.5B from Cmnd 9702 derive from two major factors only: first, the effect of depressed oil prices on NCB revenues, through the operation of fossil fuel market forces; and, second, the need to devote more resources, post-Chernobyl, to research and development in non-nuclear power generation technologies.   On the first issue, I propose that electricity consumers should receive the benefit of lower fossil fuel prices, consistent with the NCB continuing to be able to make progress towards elimination of its subsidy.   On the second issue, while further development of nuclear power remains a desirable objective, expectations are now that additional non-nuclear generating capacity will be needed in the medium term, and I therefore propose that work on new fossil fuel technologies, renewable sources and other options should be brought forward.

2.   Detailed changes are as follows:

(i)   A reduction of £3m is forecast in the 1986/87 outturn for selective assistance, compared with Cmnd 9702. This arises from the expected decrease in take-up of grants under the Coal Firing Scheme because of the increased attractiveness of oil firing at current world oil prices.

(ii)   The NCB's EFL in 1986/87 is expected to increase by £250m, compared with Cmnd 9702. This reflects reduced revenues from sales to CEGB arising from the coal price deal recently concluded between the two Boards. The deal is worth £280-£300m to CEGB in 1987/88 (to be passed on to consumers through reduced prices), but the NCB's EFL assumes some internal savings.

(iii)   I propose that non-nuclear research and development expenditure should be progressively increased until it reaches a level of about £100m p.a. at the end of the decade, approximately twice the level assumed in Cmnd 9702. This will still leave the total well below expenditure on nuclear research and also well below the current levels of expenditure, on renewables in particular, by other countries. Additional resources need now to be committed to the following:

(a)   Severn and Mersey Barrage feasibility studies. Barrages have potential to make an important contribution to power supplies in the future. While it is primarily for the CEGB and potential constructors and their backers to assess the technical and financial feasibility of the project, complex environmental, planning and political issues, inevitably involving government, will also have to be overcome. Government should therefore act as a partner in continuing studies, partly to demonstrate the will to co-operate in solving these issues if the project proves to be technically and financially viable, and partly to ensure the ground is prepared in the best possible way before any decision to launch the project is taken.

(b)   Pressure to install Flue Gas Desulphurisation (FGD) on existing or new fossil fuel power stations is growing. CEGB has a programme of research and development in hand. However, FGD, if fitted, will produce considerable quantities of waste products, some of which will impact on existing markets for chemicals. Technical and economic studies of a wide-ranging nature are required.

(c)   New coal burning technology. Government should share in the programme being conducted by the CEGB and NCB into Pressurised Fluidised Bed Combustion, as a means of influencing its future development. It should also, as part of the same programme or separately, encourage further work on coal gasification.

(d)   Extension of research into geothermal energy by development of deeper boreholes.

(e)   Adoption of large diameter windmill projects for further development.

(f)   Additional promotional activities to assist adoption of solar power equipment, and to encourage conservation.

(iv)   Again, the NCB's EFL in 1987/88 is expected to increase by some £250m compared with Cmnd 9702 as a consequence of the two-year deal (1986/87-87/88) recently concluded with the CEGB. As in 1986/87, the cost of the NCB is put at some £300m, partially offset by internal savings.

(v)   There is no firm agreement with the CEGB beyond 1987/88, but

99

NCB coal prices are not expected to show real increases in the period 1988/90. During these latter years, however, NCB cost savings may be expected progressively to compensate for reduction in revenue.

TABLE 7.5A   DEPARTMENT OF ENERGY

	1986/87 Expend. (Cmnd 9702)	1987/88 Revised Plan	Absolute Change 1987/88- 1986/87	Percent Change 1987/88- 1986/87
	£m	£m	£m	%
CURRENT GOVERNMENT Voted in Estimates				
4.1 Selective assistance to individual firms and undertakings	26	20	(6)	(23)
4.1 Other support services	6	10	4	67
4.2 Research and development				
- Non nuclear	45	60	15	33
- Nuclear	181	200	19	10
4.2 Promotion of energy efficiency	16	20	4	25
4.4 Redundant mineworkers' payments scheme	486	270	(216)	(44)
4.8 Other central and misc. services	33	30	(3)	(9)
Total Voted in Estimates	793	610	(183)	(23)
Other central government				
4.1 Other support services				
4.2 Research and development				
- Nuclear	(2)		2	(100)
TOTAL CENTRAL GOVERNMENT	791	610	(181)	(23)
PUBLIC CORPORATIONS				
4.13 Nationalised industries' EFLs				
Voted in Estimates	730	490	(240)	(33)
Other	(1,416)	(1,370)	46	(3)
Total nationalised industries' EFLs	(686)	(880)	(194)	28
4.14 Other public corporations				
Voted in Estimates				
United Kingdom Atomic Energy Authority	9	(10)	(19)	(211)
TOTAL PUBLIC CORPORATIONS	(677)	(890)	(213)	31
TOTAL DEPARTMENT OF ENERGY	114	(280)	(394)	(346)

TABLE 7.5B DEPARTMENT OF ENERGY

	1986/87 Expenditure (Cmnd 9702) £m	1986/87 Estimated Outturn £m	1987/88 Revised Plan £m	1988/89 Revised Plan £m	1989/90 Plan £m	Absolute Change 1989/90-1986/87 £m	Percentage Change 1989/90-1986/87 %
CENTRAL GOVERNMENT							
Voted in Estimates							
4.1 Selective assistance to individual firms & undertakings	26	23	20	20	20	(6)	(23)
4.1 Other support services	6	6	10	10	10	4	67
4.2 R&D: Non nuclear	45	45	60	80	100	55	122
Nuclear	181	181	200	210	220	39	22
4.2 Promotion of energy efficiency	16	16	20	20	20	4	25
4.4 Redundant mineworkers' payments scheme	486	486	270	280	300	(186)	(38)
4.8 Other central and misc. services	33	33	30	40	40	7	21
Total Voted in Estimates	793	790	610	660	710	(83)	(10)
Other central government							
4.1 Other support services							
4.2 Research and development:							
Nuclear	(2)	(2)					
TOTAL CENTRAL GOVERNMENT	791	788	610	660	710	(82)	(10)
PUBLIC CORPORATIONS							
4.13 Nationalised industries' EFL							
Voted in Estimates	730	980	490	400	200	(530)	(73)
Other	(1,416)	(1,416)	(1,370)	(1,100)	(1,200)	216	(15)
Total nat. inds' EFLs	(686)	(436)	(880)	(700)	(1,000)	(314)	(46)
4.14 Other public corporations							
Voted in Estimates							
United Kingdom Atomic Energy Authority	9	9	(10)	(10)	(10)	(19)	(211)
TOTAL PUBLIC CORPORATIONS	(677)	(427)	(890)	(710)	(1,010)	(333)	49
TOTAL DEPARTMENT OF ENERGY	114	361	(280)	(50)	(300)	(415)	(363)

7.6 Department of Employment

Mark Cornelius

1.   The most pressing economic and social problem which this Cabinet must address is unemployment. The jobless total presently stands at 3.25m, a post-war record. While this is unacceptably high, more distressing still is the fact that 1.3m or 40% of that total have been unemployed for over a year (the official definition of long-term unemployment) and that 500,000 have been unemployed for over three years.

2.   Although part of the solution lies in providing the right macroeconomic conditions for more jobs to be created, there is every reason to believe that the long-term unemployed would initially be excluded from any general recovery. This is demonstrated by the experience of the last three years. Despite the creation of 1m jobs, long-term unemployment has risen by a quarter of a million. The jobs have generally been taken by the short-term unemployed and new entrants to the labour market.

3.   There are many reasons for this phenomenon. In the first place people become discouraged from looking for work after a long spell of unemployment. To help solve this problem the Department has recently instituted a nationwide system of counselling interviews for the long-term unemployed, which should encourage and aid them in their search for work. However, despite these efforts to ameliorate the demoralisation felt by the long-term unemployed, more needs to be done to improve their prospect of finding a job. The chances of the unemployed doing it on their own are slim. Employers are often unwilling to take on long-term unemployed if they can choose someone else, for they tend to think prolonged inactivity will lead to poor motivation and deskilling.

4.   Thus, with the possibility of regular employment denied to most long-term unemployed, the public sector has a responsibility to help these people back into the labour force through the provision of socially-useful work for a limited period. This should enable them to acquire new skills and re-acquire the habit of working, which would once again put them on an equal footing in the market place.

5.   The Department of Employment, through the agency of the Manpower Services Commission, presently operates the Community Programme which is specifically tailored to such an end. The Community Programme also offers places for those under 25 who have been unemployed for more than six months. However, with a client group of 1.6m, the 255,000 places on the Community Programme do not begin to match up to the size of the problem. We believe we should aim to provide the guarantee of at least an offer of a job to all the long-term unemployed for a period of up to a year.

6.   Our proposal, which is based on extensive consultation, offers the cheapest (in terms of cost per job) and most effective way of making a significant impact on unemployment.

7.   We envisage that the provision of a job guarantee would entail the creation of 750,000 extra jobs in addition to the 255,000 places on the Community Programme.

8.   The jobs would be provided in the following areas:

(i)   *Building Improvement Programme*

Much of the fabric of our cities is in terrible disrepair. The various memoranda to the NEDC on the infrastructure have shown the size of the problem in housing, schools, hospitals and roads. In many areas expenditure today could save much larger expenditure tomorrow. The obvious possible kinds of work are:

-    external and internal decoration and renovation of houses, especially those belonging to pensioners and others on low incomes;

-    decoration and renovation of schools and hospitals;

-    minor road repairs;

-    site clearance and environmental improvements.

(ii)   *Social Services and Health*

There are obvious unmet needs in social services and health. The National Health Service is short of orderlies, cleaners, laundry and catering staff. There is also plenty of scope for extending care in the community. Present resources are a constraint. The solution should not be just to provide more money, but to provide more money linked to spending it on the long-term unemployed.

(iii)   *Private Sector*

One cannot deal with a problem of the current size without increasing private employment of the long-term unemployed in as many sectors as possible. An obvious approach is that private employers taking on long-term unemployed should receive a subsidy for the first year of their employment, provided that non-subsidised employment does not fall.

9.   We have estimated that the full-year gross cost of our proposals for the job guarantee after three years would be £5.5bn (i.e. more than the Chancellor believes he has available). However, the savings which can be made through reduced DHSS expenditure on social security benefits (approximately £1.5bn) and cuts which we have proposed in other programmes in our own budget should be enough to make the guarantee affordable within the Chancellor's constraints.

10.   Indeed, from a Treasury point of view, there are several advantages to our proposals. First, the extra tax revenue generated from bringing more people into work would mean a lower PSBR cost than is implied by the increase in expenditure. Second, the scheme does not represent a permanent addition to the Department's budget, for it will tend to be self-liquidating as the backlog of long-term unemployment is cleared. Third, as it is important that any increase in public expenditure does not lead to an upsurge in inflation, this proposal represents a safe option. It is now widely recognised that measures targeted at reducing the level of long-term unemployment are not likely to put upward pressure on wages and prices as may be the case with attempts to reduce unemployment generally.

11.   From a Cabinet point of view, this proposal should not be seen as diverting extra resources from areas where they are clearly needed. My colleagues at DES, DTp, DHSS and DoE will all benefit from the extra manpower which this proposal would provide.

12.   Some colleagues may believe that the proposals we have outlined are too ambitious. We would not deny that they represent an enormous challenge. However it is not, we believe, a challenge on which we should turn our backs. There are 1.5m people who are at present not able to discern any real hope of participating in society: they deserve our help to restore that hope.

Justification for changes

Cash increases for 1987/88 over 1986/87 are, for most categories of expenditure, small if not negative. There are three exceptions which we will seek to justify.

(a) *General Labour Market Services*

The estimated outturn for 1986/87 exceeds the plan contained in Cmnd 9702 - II by £60m. This is due to changes in the Community Programme announced in the 1986 Budget. The number of places was raised from 230,000 to 255,000 and the maximum average wage was increased from £63 to £67 per week (£60m part-year cost, £120m full-year cost).

The net cash increase in 1987/88 over 1986/87 (£594m) primarily reflects:

-      some small reductions in minor programmes (£11m part-year and full-year benefit);

-      the working through of the full-year cost of the changes to the Community Programme proposed in the 1986 Budget (£60m) and the 1986 public expenditure White Paper (£45m);

-      an increase in the maximum average salary paid to those on the Community Programme from £67 a week to £105 a week (£0.5bn part-year and full-year cost).

This latter increase reflects a policy change. As the rules governing the Community Programme stipulate that the projects should pay the going rate for the job, the agencies who run them are finding it increasingly difficult to provide full-time jobs at such a low wage. Consequently, 80% of jobs covered by the Community Programme are part-time. Moreover, a wage of £67 a week effectively excludes anybody who needs to support a family. As a result, two-thirds of those on the Community Programme are under 25. To improve the balance of the coverage and to increase the availability of full-time jobs, we propose that the maximum average salary be increased.

(b) *Promotion and Preservation of Employment Opportunities, Compensation Payments etc.*

The estimated outturn for 1986/87 exceeds the plan contained in Cmnd 9702 - II by £125m. This is due to:

- the introduction of the New Workers' Scheme (NWS) in the 1986 Budget, which is a job subsidy to employers designed to encourage them to take on young people coming off the YTS (£25m part-year cost, £50m full-year cost);

- the introduction of the Restart Programme, which involves payment of a subsidy to the long-term unemployed to take low-paid work plus intensive counselling to help and encourage the long-term unemployed to look for jobs (£100m part-year cost, full-year cost not relevant).

The net cash increase in 1987/88 over 1986/87 (£1334m) primarily reflects:

- the working through of the full-year cost of the NWS (£25m);

- the ending of the Job Start Allowance which is part of the Restart Programme (£100m). The counselling side of the Restart initiative and those already receiving a Job Start Allowance will be catered for within our job guarantee (see below);

- the introduction of the job guarantee (£1.5bn part-year cost, £5.1bn full-year cost - see General Remarks);

- a reduction in the provision of the Job Release Scheme (JRS) and Job Splitting Scheme (JSS) (£91m part-year benefit, £146m full-year benefit).

This last policy change reflects a decision to phase out the JRS and JSS over a two year period. Such schemes are based on the fallacy that we have to share out a limited amount of work. With so much work needing to be done this seems to us inappropriate. Resources should not be spent on encouraging people to do *less* work in order to provide opportunities for the unemployed.

(c)   *Manpower Services Commission*

The estimated outturn for 1986 exceeds the plan contained in Cmnd 9702 - II by £5m. This is due to the extra provision of resources for the Enterprise Allowance Scheme in the 1986 budget (£5m part-year cost, £35m full-year cost).

The net cash increase in 1987/88 over 1986/87 (£210m) primarily reflects:

-   the working through of the full-year cost of increased provision for the Enterprise Allowance Scheme as outlined in the 1986 budget (£30m) and the 1986 public expenditure White Paper (£19m);

-   the working through of the full-year cost of the extension of the YTS from a one to a two-year scheme (£171m);

-   some small reductions in other programmes (£10m part-year and full-year benefit).

TABLE 7.6A   DEPARTMENT OF EMPLOYMENT

	1986/87 Expend. (Cmnd 9702)	1987/88 Revised Plan	Absolute Change 1987/88-1986/87	Percent Change 1987/88-1986/87
	£m	£m	£m	%
CENTRAL GOVERNMENT				
Voted in Estimates				
4.1 Promotion of tourism	40	40	0	0
4.1 Small firms etc. support services	13	10	(3)	(23)
4.7 General labour market services	1,086	1,740	654	60
4.7 Careers service grant	1		(1)	(100)
4.7 Services for seriously disabled people	67	70	3	4
4.7 Promotion and preservation of employment opportunities, compensationpayments, etc.	146	1,605	1,459	999
4.8 Central services	52	50	(2)	(4)
4.7 Advisory Conciliation and Arb. Service	15	20	5	33
4.9 Health & Safety Commission	94	100	6	6
4.7 Manpower Services Commission	1,820	2,035	215	12
Total Voted in Estimates	3,334	5,670	2,336	70
Other central government				
4.1 Small firms etc. support services				
4.7 Redundancy & Maternity Pay Funds	303	180	(123)	(41)
4.8 Central services				
4.7 Manpower Services Commission				
TOTAL CENTRAL GOVERNMENT	3,637	5,850	2,213	61
LOCAL AUTHORITIES				
Relevant current spending				
4.7 Careers service	57	60	3	5
4.7 Services for seriously disabled people	27	30	3	11
Total relevant current spending	84	90	6	7
Non relevant current spending				
4.7 Careers service	13	10	(3)	(23)
4.7 Manpower Services Commission				
Local authority capital				
4.7 Careers service				
4.7 Services for seriously disabled people	5		(5)	(100)
4.7 Manpower Services Commission				
TOTAL LOCAL AUTHORITIES	102	100	(2)	(2)
PUBLIC CORPORATIONS				
4.14 Other public corporations				
National Dock Labour Board	4		(4)	(100)
Voted in Estimates				
Other				
TOTAL PUBLIC CORPORATIONS	4		(4)	(100)
TOTAL DEPARTMENT OF EMPLOYMENT	3,743	5,950	2,207	59

TABLE 7.6B   DEPARTMENT OF EMPLOYMENT

	1986/87 Expenditure (Cmnd 9702) £m	1986/87 Estimated Outturn £m	1987/88 Revised Plan £m	1988/89 Revised Plan £m	1989/90 Plan £m	Absolute Change 1989/90-1986/87 £m	Percentage Change 1989/90-1986/87 %
CENTRAL GOVERNMENT							
Voted in Estimates							
4.1 Promotion of tourism	40	40	40	40	40	0	0
4.1 Small firms etc. support services	13	13	10	10	10	(3)	(23)
4.7 General labour market services	1,086	1,146	1,740	1,760	1,812	726	67
4.7 Careers service grant		1				(1)	(100)
4.7 Services for seriously disabled people	67	67	70	70	70	3	4
4.7 Promotion and preservation of employment opportunities, compensation payments etc.	146	271	1,605	3,550	5,550	5,404	3,701
4.8 Central services	52	52	50	60	60	8	15
4.7 Advisory Conciliation and Arb. Service	15	15	20	20	20	5	33
4.9 Health & Safety Commission	94	94	100	100	100	6	6
4.7 Manpower Services Commission	1,820	1,825	2,035	2,175	2,240	420	23
Total Voted in Estimates	3,334	3,524	5,670	7,785	9,902	6,568	197
Other central government							
4.7 Redundancy & Maternity Pay Funds	303	303	180	190	190	(113)	(37)
TOTAL CENTRAL GOVERNMENT	3,637	3,827	5,850	7,975	10,092	6,455	177
LOCAL AUTHORITIES							
Relevant current spending							
4.7 Careers Service	57	57	60	60	60	3	5
4.7 Services for seriously disabled people	27	27	30	30	30	3	11
Total relevant current spending	84	84	90	90	90	6	7
Non relevant current spending							
4.7 Careers service	13	13	10	10	10	(3)	(23)
Local authority capital							
4.7 Services for seriously disabled people	5	5				(5)	(100)
TOTAL LOCAL AUTHORITIES	102	102	100	100	100	(2)	(2)
PUBLIC CORPORATIONS							
National Dock Labour Board	4	4				(4)	(100)
TOTAL PUBLIC CORPORATIONS	4	4				(4)	(100)
TOTAL DEPT. OF EMPLOYMENT	3,743	3,933	5,950	8,075	10,192	6,449	172

7.7 Department of Transport

Stephen Glaister

1.   An increase above the 1986 White Paper (Cmnd 9702) expenditure level is planned on maintenance and reconstruction of local and trunk roads. This is to rectify the accelerating deterioration due to neglect over the last decade while taking advantage of current low road construction costs. Some extra new road construction is planned towards the end of the period. Modest extra resources are planned for revenue and capital purposes in the local bus industry outside the metropolitan areas in recognition of the loss of cross-subsidy due to deregulation. A proportion of this is financed by a continued reduction in the requirement for external finance for the public corporations, especially by British Rail and London Regional Transport.

2.   By the end of the plan, Transport's proportion of the total is 3.51%, which is slightly higher than the Cmnd 9702 plan of 3.24% for 1988/89, but still considerably below the proportion in 1978-85 (4.04% declining to 3.54%). In many cases an explicit estimate is available of the economic return to marginal expenditure. This is typically between £1.40 and £1.75 per £1 spent. Real rates of return are typically 10-14% p.a.

Roads

3.   Road transport is far and away the most important of the transport sectors. All expenditure on provision and maintenance of the fixed infrastructure appears as a contribution to public expenditure plans. Car ownership grew by 25% in the last decade, and the official traffic forecasts (1984 revision), which I believe to be somewhat over-cautious, show sustained growth of car traffic of 0.5 - 2% p.a., assuming GDP growth of 1 - 2%. Since these forecasts were prepared there are grounds for more optimism concerning fuel prices and GDP. Freight ton-miles are expected to be more stable, but the average weight of lorries is expected to continue to increase, which will make disproportionate demands on the standards of road maintenance.

4.   Capacity on the motorway and trunk road networks seems to be generally adequate until the turn of the century. However, London and some other major urban areas are exceptions to this. Further, there are already capacity problems on local roads (which comprise 96% by length

of the network). The economic and environmental case has been established for several hundred new local bypass and relief road schemes. Economic benefits are typically £1.50 to £1.75 per £1 of expenditure. An important consideration is that the Road Construction Price Index has remained stagnant (in nominal terms) since 1980, due to depression in the construction industry. One cannot expect this to continue indefinitely and it is sensible to exploit the situation while generating some new employment in the industry.

5.   Although a large number of these schemes has already been designed in detail, statutory procedure means that they cannot be started immediately. On the national roads construction programme, I have allowed for an extra 5% real increase in 1988/89 and a further 10% real increase in 1989/90. This would achieve of the order of 130 extra single carriageway-miles in the final year. For local authority new construction I have allowed an extra £50m in 1987/88 and in 1988/89. For the final year the 1988/89 level is maintained in real terms, with the further addition of £100m.

6.   Structural renewal and maintenance of roads has become an altogether more pressing problem. Fortunately, it is easier to achieve increased rates of spending quickly. The National Road Condition Survey has shown a steady deterioration since 1980, but the 1985 survey, published after Cmnd 9702, shows a sudden, and statistically significant worsening. This is consistent with the deflection survey which is more thorough but has a narrower coverage. The greatest problems appear to be occurring with rural unclassified roads and, much more importantly, urban principal and trunk roads.

7.   It was estimated in 1983 that 22% of the trunk and 34% of urban principal road network had a residual life under 10 years. Motorway reconstruction has been keeping pace, but trunk and principal road reconstruction has not. A procession of select committees and other official investigations have recommended an increase in maintenance and renewal expenditures.

8.   Cmnd 9702 gives no new allowance for current national maintenance expenditure. I have increased it by 15% in real terms for 1987/88. The additional allowance in Cmnd 9702 for structural renewal of trunks is inadequate. For 1987/88, I have increased it by the £30m necessary to 'stand still' plus the £23m p.a. necessary to eliminate the outstanding backlog on trunk roads over three years. This addition is held constant in real terms over the remaining years.

9.   For local roads maintenance, Cmnd 9702 gives the bare minimum requirement of a 10% real increase for 1986/87. I have further increased this by 5% real for 1987/88 and maintained the level in real terms thereafter.

10.   The economic and engineering analysis of road maintenance expenditure would repay further development. It is difficult to state precise rates of return. One (not entirely disinterested) authority claims that expenditure is recouped in terms of reduced vehicle repair and accident costs alone. Given the progressive nature of the deterioration of an unrepaired road, it would seem sensible to avoid long-standing maintenance backlogs: the Department estimated in 1984 that 40% of structural maintenance requirement was due to backlogs and this is three times more expensive than overlay which could have been carried out quickly.

Special initiatives

11.   I have separately identified planned expenditure on five new initiatives.

12.   The tolling of existing crossings such as the Severn Bridge is an anomaly in the British highway system leading to inefficient usage. The abolition of tolls in England would have a net revenue cost of about £30m p.a. (This is insufficient to fund the corresponding debt - whether found by toll or by other means, and it would seem sensible to seek a means of writing it off.)

13.   There is a wide measure of agreement that exceptional rates of return can be obtained by small-scale expenditures on road accident investigation and prevention (AIP schemes). It seems that there has been insufficient initiative within local authorities to win funds from competing claims. Experimentally £20m p.a. is provided for earmarked grants for this purpose.

14.   Traffic and parking enforcement in London has reached an impasse. I propose the creation of a new enforcement corps on the Washington model, as developed by the GLC. Subject to resolution of the legal difficulties, I would expect London Regional Transport to be responsible. Costing is difficult since it depends upon any attributed savings achieved on the present Warden and Police forces, and on penalty revenues. I have allowed £5m as a set-up cost and an annual running cost of £20m, constant in real terms.

15.   Deregulation of buses in October 1986 will destroy the extensive

system of finance by internal cross-subsidy. So far no provision has been made to replace this with external subsidy (save the rural bus grant, which I now intend to maintain throughout the planning period). The Government's expectation is that cost reductions under competition will be sufficient to maintain the bulk of services. This is likely to be so in the case of the metropolitan areas where subsidy levels have been high. However, there is a large number of urban and semi-rural areas with bus operators which are already efficiently run with little or no subsidy and which will fall outside the scope of rural bus grant. A new grant of £40m p.a. is proposed to deal with cases of undue hardship in such circumstances. It may be appropriate for the Traffic Commissioners to administer this through a system of competitive tender. Economic returns of about £1.20 - £1.40 per £1 spent have been estimated for urban bus subsidy, providing none of it is dissipated in reduced efficiency.

16.   I assume that the commitment to deregulate buses in London will be carried out. I have therefore taken £100m from what London Regional Transport's EFL would otherwise have been and entered it here. LRT will cease to give London Buses direct subsidy and will administer this sum so as to secure unremunerative services by open tender. London Buses will be free to bid, as in the system of route tendering presently operated by LRT. Since this item is transferred from the EFL it does not affect the public expenditure planning total.

Local authorities

17.   With the exception of roads maintenance and expenditures already discussed, local authority expenditures are much the same as planned in Cmnd 9702, in so far as the latter can be ascertained. A progressive real reduction in support for the bus industry is implied - very largely in the metropolitan areas which consume most of it. However, revenue support and concessionary fares is the one item where the 1986/87 outturn will be significantly different from Cmnd 9702. Current expenditure outturn is estimated at about £1860m as against the plan of £1747m. If achieved, then the plans for 1987/88 would represent a much more severe decline in these items relative to the 1986 outturn.

Public corporations

18.   After some investment in the early years, the British Airports Authority is assumed successfully privatised. Likewise, the Civil Aviation Authority has some early investment, but is then planned to set its charges so as to break even by 1989/90.

19.   The expected 1986/87 profit for the National Bus Company now looks optimistic and the outturn is written down to break even.

20.   Cmnd 9702 sets a tough EFL for the British Railways Board in 1986/87. It is assumed that this will be met and that it would have been further tightened in 1987/88 were it not for a peak in the investment requirements in that year. The EFL is reduced in cash terms in 1988/89 and again in 1989/90 in line with reducing investment requirements and further pressure on unit costs. It may be considered necessary - and desirable - to relieve the railways of some of their Public Service Obligations in order to meet these targets, or better them.

21.   For all three years, London Regional Transport's EFL is reduced by £100m to offset the London deregulation grant (paragraph 16). Taking this into account, falling unit costs and buoyant revenues would have allowed the EFL to reduce from £300m in 1987/88 to £253m in 1989/90. However, traffic on London Underground has increased by over 35% since 1983 and it is predicted to continue growing by 2% p.a. for the next few years. This has created a severe shortage of capacity in places requiring additional investment in rolling stock of £15m in 1987/88 and 1988/89, and £30m in 1989/90.

TABLE 7.7A   DEPARTMENT OF TRANSPORT

	1986/87 Expend. (Cmnd 9702) £m	1987/88 Revised Plan £m	Absolute Change 1987/88-1986/87 £m	Percent Change 1987/88-1986/87 %
CENTRAL GOVERNMENT				
Voted in Estimates				
6.1 National roads systems				
- Current maintenance	82	95	13	16
- Structural maintenance	151	212	61	40
- New construction	665	690	25	4
6.3 Bus grants	20	40	20	100
6.3 Freight facilities grants	6	10	4	67
6.3 BR pensions and other	95	90	(5)	(5)
6.3 NFC pensions	8	10	2	25
6.4 Ports	17	10	(7)	(41)
6.4 Shipping services	48	50	2	4
6.6 Civil aviation services	8	6	(2)	(25)
6.7 Roads and transport administration	57	63	6	11
6.7 Licensing & testing	18	25	7	39
6.7 Research and development	22	25	3	14
6.7 Road safety	8	10	2	25
6.7 International subscriptions etc.	1	0	(1)	(100)
6.8 Driver and vehicle licensing	111	115	4	4
6.4 Civil defence	2	0	(2)	(100)
Initiatives				
Tolled crossings		30	30	
Accident Investigation & Prevention grant		20	20	
London traffic enforcement agency		25	25	
Non-rural, non-Met. bus grant		40	40	
London deregulation grant		100	100	
Total Voted in Estimates	1,319	1,666	347	26
Other				
6.4 Ports	(11)	(10)	1	(9)
TOTAL - CENTRAL GOVERNMENT	1,308	1,656	348	27
LOCAL AUTHORITIES				
6.2 Roads maintenance	1,115	1,272	157	14
Revenue support & concessionary fares	447	400	(47)	(11)
Other	185	185	0	0
Total	1,747	1,857	110	6
6.2 Capital - Roads	533	603	70	13
- Trading services	99	97	(2)	(2)
Total	632	700	68	11
TOTAL - LOCAL AUTHORITIES	2,379	2,557	178	7
PUBLIC CORPORATIONS				
6.5 British Airports Authority	15	0	(15)	(100)
British Railways Board	771	770	(1)	(0)
National Bus Company	(13)	0	13	(100)
Civil Aviation Authority	14	10	(4)	(29)
London Regional Transport	304	214	(90)	(30)
Total - nationalised industries' EFLs	1,091	994	(97)	(9)
6.9 Other public corporations	34	30	(4)	(12)
TOTAL - PUBLIC CORPORATIONS	1,125	1,024	(101)	(9)
TOTAL DEPARTMENT OF TRANSPORT	4,812	5,237	425	9

TABLE 7.7B DEPARTMENT OF TRANSPORT

	1986/87 Expend. (Cmnd 9702) £m	1986/87 Estimated Outturn £m	1987/88 Revised Plan £m	1988/89 Revised Plan £m	1989/90 Plan £m	Absolute Change 1989/90- 1986/87 £m	Percent Change 1989/90- 1986/87 %
CENTRAL GOVERNMENT							
6.1 National roads systems							
Current maintenance	82	82	95	99	102	20	24
Structural maintenance	151	151	212	219	226	75	50
New construction	665	665	690	750	850	185	28
6.3 Bus grants	20	20	40	40	40	20	100
6.3 Freight facilities grants	6	6	10	10	10	4	67
6.3 BR pensions and other	95	95	90	100	103	8	8
6.3 NFC pensions	8	8	10	10	10	2	25
6.4 Ports	17	17	10	0	0	(17)	(100)
6.4 Shipping services	48	48	50	50	50	2	4
6.6 Civil aviation services	8	8	6	3	0	(8)	(100)
6.7 Roads and transport administration	57	57	63	65	67	10	18
6.7 Licensing and testing	18	18	25	21	21	3	17
6.7 Research and development	22	22	25	26	27	5	23
6.7 Road safety	8	8	10	10	11	3	38
6.7 International subscriptions etc.	1	1	0	0	0	(1)	(100)
6.8 Driver and vehicle licensing	111	111	115	119	123	12	11
9.4 Civil defence	2	2	0	0	0	(2)	(100)
Initiatives							
Tolled crossings			30	32	32	32	
Accident Investigation and Prevention Grant			20	21	21	21	
London traffic enforcement agency			25	21	21	21	
Non-rural, non-Met. bus grant			40	40	40	40	
London deregulation grant			100	100	100	100	
Total Voted in Estimates	1,319	1,319	1,666	1,735	1,854	535	41

Contd

TABLE 7.7B DEPARTMENT OF TRANSPORT (Continued)

	1986/87 Expend. (Cmnd 9702) £m	1986/87 Estimated Outturn £m	1987/88 Revised Plan £m	1988/89 Revised Plan £m	1989/90 Plan £m	Absolute Change 1989/90-1986/87 £m	Percent Change 1989/90-1986/87 %
CENTRAL GOVERNMENT (Continued)							
Other							
6.4 Ports	(11)	(11)	(10)	(10)	(10)	1	(9)
TOTAL – CENTRAL GOVERNMENT	1,308	1,308	1,656	1,725	1,844	536	41
LOCAL AUTHORITIES							
6.2 Roads maintenance	1,115	1,115	1,272	1,317	1,357	242	22
Revenue support and concessionary fares	447	562	400	400	400	(47)	(11)
Other	185	185	185	185	185	0	0
Total	1,747	1,862	1,857	1,902	1,942	195	11
6.2 Capital							
Roads	533	533	603	622	741	208	39
Trading services	99	129	97	108	111	12	12
Total	632	662	700	730	852	220	35
TOTAL – LOCAL AUTHORITIES	2,379	2,524	2,557	2,632	2,794	415	17
PUBLIC CORPORATIONS							
6.5 British Airports Authority	15	15	0	0	0	(15)	(100)
British Railways Board	771	771	770	710	700	(71)	(9)
National Bus Company	(13)	0	0	0	0	13	(100)
Civil Aviation Authority	14	14	10	5	0	(14)	(100)
London Regional Transport	304	304	214	222	183	(121)	(40)
Total – nat. inds' EFLs	1,091	1,108	994	937	883	(208)	(19)
6.9 Other public corporations	34	34	30	30	30	(4)	(12)
TOTAL – PUBLIC CORPORATIONS	1,129	1,142	1,024	967	913	(212)	(19)
TOTAL – DEPARTMENT OF TRANSPORT	4,812	4,974	5,237	5,324	5,551	739	15

7.8 Department of the Environment

George Jones

Opening statement

1.   We must bring to an end the annual embarrassment for the Government of local government exceeding government plans for expenditure. Realism should be brought into our estimating, otherwise our figures lose credibility. We know that our figures will never be met and they have to be revised for realism each year. But they provoke considerable conflict with local government which rightly claims that we expect harsher cuts from its expenditure than from expenditure under our direct control. This confrontation with local government is damaging to our political prospects, and it is unnecessary.

2.   The answer is simple: to remove from our plans local government expenditure financed by local tax. There is no economic reason to include it. It does not affect money supply or public sector borrowing requirement, and has only a small impact, if any, on interest rates and inflation. No other comparable country includes such local spending in its national process of expenditure allocation, and none suffers economic mishaps from not doing so. The figures were first included in the 1960s as forecasting estimates but later became transformed into control targets. We should concentrate on getting our own expenditure under control. For that we are responsible.

3.   My tables exclude local government expenditure financed from local tax and focus on expenditure under my control. Other departments should do the same. We need to decide as a Government on the total grant we will set for local government. Accordingly, I present a set of four tables: 7.8C and 7.8D (equivalent to other table As and Bs respectively); and two new tables for central government grant to local authorities in 1987/88 and 1989/90 (Tables 7.8E and 7.8F respectively). Table 7.8F begins with an estimate of total grant for 1986/87, calculated from the various grants for local authorities, and from that base it projects forward to 1989/90 assuming an increase in total relevant expenditure of 5-6% a year and a stable grant of 45% on that expenditure. I urge colleagues to pay attention to the 1986/87 figure for estimated expenditure rather than the figure from Cmnd 9702, which was unrealistic. It has been adjusted

for realism by about 9% to take account of two teachers' pay settlements, the shift in local elections away from Conservative control in 1985 and 1986, and changes in grant. These circumstances should not occur in the future, so, with a fall in inflation, it is wise to plot a lower annual increase in total relevant expenditure.

4.   I have made allowance in my grant for the abolition of specific grants, namely for the Urban Programme and Derelict Land Reclamation. As the Minister responsible for the health of local government I am opposed to the specific grant. It raises my departmental costs through having staff crawl over local government's activities. There is no evidence that these trendy grants have a beneficial effect. They should be merged into the general grant, thus allowing local authorities which understand local conditions to spend it according to their judgement. In similar vein I have abolished regional and general industrial support. It is unnecessary, going largely to business that would have taken the same decisions without the aid. It sustains the Development Commission, a quango, whose activities should soon cease. As believers in democratic accountability we should seek to eliminate such appointed boards, or reduce their role.

5.   I propose increases in expenditure on royal palaces and parks, and historic buildings, since they help our tourist earnings. Such a programme fits in with our campaign to make Britain a more attractive place to live in. Also, Hampton Court will have to be restored.

6.   I have reduced expenditure on grants to environmental bodies. They are either unnecessary or should seek funding more from the private sector.

7.   I have reduced expenditure on departmental administration; it will arise from staff savings from the reduction in central controls following the abolition of specific grants, a less nannying culture in the department, simplification of the Rate Support Grant system, and the beneficial results of the Financial Management Initiative, so much urged by the Prime Minister.

8.   I have maintained research on the environment and raised that on water, accepting previous plans.

9.   I have accepted, too, previous plans for nationalised industries' EFLs and for receipts from New Towns, but I have reduced provision for the Urban Development Corporations. The private sector is best fitted to decide on industrial location; if our pump-priming and scene-setting is appropriate then they will act. To increase spending here would be a

waste of public money.

10.   Overall, I have reduced departmental spending on 'other environmental services', both in 1987/88 on 1986/87, and longer term in 1989/90 on 1986/87.

11.   On housing, I have increased capital spending and reduced current spending. I see no economic justification for continued subsidies to rents. The market is distorted. There is no social reason, either. In the long term, cheaper accommodation will become available from the private sector after subsidies go. I plan not a disruptive abolition, but a phased withdrawal. The increase in capital spending is important to replenish our housing stock, to give a boost to the building industry, and thus reduce unemployment. It is a highly visible product, with great electoral appeal; those likely to be temporarily hurt by the decrease in rent subsidies would have been unlikely to vote for us in any case. A large house-building programme could be a major election winner. And I have obtained the increase in capital spending on housing within reduced totals for both my housing expenditure plans as a whole and my 'other environmental services' plan in the short and long term.

Fall-back position

12.   Colleagues have decided not to take radical action and have left me with the task of having to include figures for local government expenditure, even if financed by local taxation. So, I now present my second set of tables (Tables 7.8A and 7.8B). They embody for my departmental expenditure the same approach I outlined in my first commentary on the first set of tables. They begin with a realistic base for local spending, in order to put an end to the confrontation over unrealistic targets. They assume the abolition of specific grants, a reduction in provision for quangos, a decrease in departmental administration, acceptance of previous plans for water services and research on water and the environment, and for nationalised industries' EFLs and New Town receipts. They contain increases for royal palaces, parks and historic buildings, and, with housing, an increase in capital spending and a cut in current, especially subsidies.

13.   If I have to include local government spending, then I have adjusted it for realism, and, with local environmental services, raised it in line with inflation plus some extra. This increase is justified by the pressing need to clean up the environment, as the Prime Minister has urged. This function is one of the earliest of local government, a

fundamental task that only a public authority can provide. It takes us back to Victorian values. Local government can do more to help industry and commerce by providing an attractive environment than by pumping in direct subsidies. It is investment for the future and will help to reduce unemployment with highly visible results that should have a major electoral appeal. I have increased capital expenditure here.

14. For local authority rate collection I have kept a squeeze to encourage efficiency, though if we move to poll tax and run it in conjunction with rates I will probably have to come back for a higher allocation. I have adopted a similar approach with local authority administration on housing. I have accepted previous plans for records and registration of vital statistics.

15. Like my colleagues, I want to encourage local authorities to privatise. However, our experience has shown that the way not to do it is by cutting their expenditure. It has not led them to privatise. If we wish to push ahead with privatisation, we must have a specific policy for that objective and not seek it indirectly through squeezing local government expenditure. I urge colleagues to be realistic. That is the main theme of my submission.

16. Overall, in 'other environmental services' I have achieved a creditable small increase in expenditure between 1986/87 and 1989/90 of 6%, and in the short term between 1986/87 and 1987/88 a reduction of 2%. While in housing, I have achieved an increase in the long and short terms of about 25%, but within that increase a major shift from current to capital, with the former falling and the latter rising, both on a large scale.

17. A final point about the need for realism: if we are so rash as to include local government spending in our process, the opposition parties in an election will pounce on our public expenditure White Paper to expose our plans for public expenditure. If we have set totally unrealistic targets for local government services we will be pilloried for seeking drastic cuts in public services. Realism will be to our electoral advantage.

TABLE 7.8A   DEPARTMENT OF THE ENVIRONMENT (FALL BACK)

	1986/87 Expend. (Cmnd 9702)	1987/88 Revised Plan	Absolute Change 1987/88- 1986/87	Percent Change 1987/88- 1986/87
	£m	£m	£m	%
Housing				
Gross capital expenditure	3,253	4,050	797	25
Capital receipts	(1,601)	(1,550)	51	3
Net capital expenditure	1,652	2,500	848	51
Current expenditure				
7.1 Subsidies for revenue deficits	911	711	(200)	(22)
7.6 Housing associations	23	23	0	0
7.6 Local authority administration	166	182	16	10
Total current expenditure	1,100	916	(184)	(17)
TOTAL - DoE - HOUSING	2,752	3,416	664	24
Other Environmental Services				
8.2 Local environmental services excluding Urban Programme:				
- Current expenditure	2,415	2,650	235	10
- Capital expenditure	205	305	100	49
8.2 Local authority rate collection	164	174	10	6
8.2 Records and registration of vital statistics	16	17	1	6
8.8 Urban Programme	227	0	(227)	(100)
8.2 Derelict land reclamation	78	0	(78)	(100)
8.5 Regional and general industrial support	27	0	(27)	(100)
8.3 Royal palaces and parks	37	40	3	8
8.4 Historic buildings	74	79	5	7
8.6 Grants to environmental bodies	95	97	2	2
8.6 Departmental administration	100	95	(5)	(5)
8.6 Environmental research	40	40	0	0
8.1 Water research and services	7	10	3	43
8.1 Nationalised industries' EFLs	138	30	(108)	(78)
8.9 Public corporations - Urban Development Corporations	82	72	(10)	(12)
- New Towns	(82)	(60)	22	27
TOTAL - DoE - OTHER ENVIRONMENTAL SERVICES	3,623	3,549	(74)	(2)
TOTAL DEPARTMENT OF THE ENVIRONMENT	6,375	6,965	590	9

TABLE 7.8B   DEPARTMENT OF THE ENVIRONMENT (FALL BACK)

	1986/87 Expenditure (Cmnd 9702) £m	1986/87 Estimated Outturn £m	1987/88 Revised Plan £m	1988/89 Revised Plan £m	1989/90 Plan £m	Absolute Change 1989/90-1986/87 £m	Percentage Change 1989/90-1986/87 %
Housing							
Gross capital expenditure	3,253	3,951	4,050	4,200	4,350	1,097	34
Capital receipts	(1,601)	(1,601)	(1,550)	(1,500)	(1,450)	151	9
Net capital expenditure	1,652	2,350	2,500	2,700	2,900	1,248	76
Current expenditure							
7.1 Subsidies for revenue deficits	911	911	711	511	311	(600)	(66)
7.6 Housing associations	23	23	23	24	25	2	9
7.6 Local authority administration	166	175	182	188	194	28	17
Total current expenditure	1,100	1,109	916	723	530	(570)	(52)
TOTAL - DoE - HOUSING	2,752	3,459	3,416	3,423	3,430	678	25
Other Environmental Services							
8.2 Local environ.serv.exc.Urban Prog.							
Current expenditure							
Capital expenditure	2,415	2,500	2,650	2,750	2,900	485	20
8.2 Local authority rate collection	205	490	305	320	335	130	63
8.2 Records and registration of vital statistics	164	168	174	180	185	21	13
8.8 Urban programme	16	16	17	18	19	3	19
8.2 Derelict land reclamation	227	227	0	0	0	(227)	(100)
8.5 Regional and general industrial support	78	78	0	0	0	(78)	(100)
8.3 Royal palaces and parks	27	27	0	0	0	(27)	(100)
8.4 Historic buildings	74	74	40	42	44	7	19
8.6 Grants to environmental bodies	95	95	79	84	90	16	22
8.6 Departmental administration	100	100	97	99	100	5	5
8.6 Environmental research	40	40	95	90	85	(15)	(15)
8.1 Water research and services	7	7	40	40	40	0	0
8.1 Nationalised industries' EFL	138	138	10	10	10	3	43
8.9 Public Corps. - Urban Dev.Corps	82	82	30	30	30	(108)	(78)
- New Towns	(82)	(82)	72	62	52	(30)	(37)
			(60)	(50)	(40)	42	51
TOTAL-DoE-OTHER ENVIRONMENTAL SERVICES	3,623	3,997	3,549	3,675	3,850	227	6
TOTAL DEPARTMENT OF THE ENVIRONMENT	6,375	7,456	6,965	7,098	7,280	905	14

TABLE 7.8C DEPARTMENT OF THE ENVIRONMENT (OPENING STATEMENT)

	1986/87 Expend. (Cmnd 9702)	1987/88 Revised Plan	Absolute Change 1987/88- 1986/87	Percent Change 1987/88- 1986/87
	£m	£m	£m	%
Housing				
Gross capital expenditure	721	755	34	5
Capital receipts	(166)	(155)	11	7
Net capital expenditure	555	600	45	8
Current expenditure				
7.1 Subsidies for revenue deficits	911	711	(200)	(22)
7.6 Housing associations	23	23	0	0
Total current expenditure	934	734	(200)	(21)
TOTAL - DoE - HOUSING	1,489	1,334	(155)	(10)
Other Environmental Services				
8.8 Urban Programme	227	0	(227)	(100)
8.2 Derelict land reclamation	78	0	(78)	(100)
8.5 Regional and general industrial support	27	0	(27)	(100)
8.3 Royal palaces and parks	37	40	3	8
8.4 Historic buildings	74	79	5	7
8.6 Grant to environmental bodies	95	97	2	2
8.6 Departmental administration	100	95	(5)	(5)
8.6 Environmental research	40	40	0	0
8.1 Water research and services	7	10	3	43
8.1 Nationalised industries' EFLs	138	30	(108)	(78)
8.9 Public Corporations - Urban Development Corporations	82	72	(10)	(12)
- New Towns	(82)	(60)	22	27
TOTAL - DoE - OTHER ENVIRONMENTAL SERVICES	823	403	(420)	(51)
TOTAL DEPARTMENT OF THE ENVIRONMENT	2,312	1,737	(575)	(25)

TABLE 7.8D   DEPARTMENT OF THE ENVIRONMENT (OPENING STATEMENT)

	1986/87 Expenditure (Cmnd 9702)	1986/87 Estimated Outturn	1987/88 Revised Plan	1988/89 Revised Plan	1989/90 Plan	Absolute Change 1989/90-1986/87	Percentage Change 1989/90-1986/87
	£m	£m	£m	£m	£m	£m	%
Housing							
Gross capital expenditure	721	721	755	795	835	114	16
Capital receipts	(166)	(166)	(155)	(145)	(135)	31	23
Net capital expenditure	555	555	600	650	700	145	26
Current expenditure							
7.1 Subsidies for revenue deficits	911	911	711	511	311	(600)	(66)
7.6 Housing associations	23	23	23	24	25	2	9
Total current expenditure	934	934	734	535	336	(598)	(64)
TOTAL - DoE - HOUSING	1,489	1,489	1,334	1,185	1,036	(453)	(30)
Other Environmental Services							
8.8 Urban Programme	227	227	0	0	0	(227)	(100)
8.2 Derelict land reclamation	78	78	0	0	0	(78)	(100)
8.5 Regional and general industrial support	27	27	0	0	0	(27)	(100)
8.3 Royal palaces and parks	37	37	40	42	44	7	19
8.4 Historic buildings	74	74	79	84	90	16	22
8.6 Grants to environmental bodies	95	95	97	99	100	5	5
8.6 Departmental administration	100	100	95	90	85	(15)	(15)
8.6 Environmental research	40	40	40	40	40	0	0
8.1 Water research and services	7	7	10	10	10	3	43
8.1 Nationalised industries' EFLs	138	138	30	30	30	(108)	(78)
8.9 Public Corporations							
- Urban Development Corporations	82	82	72	62	52	(30)	(37)
- New Towns	(82)	(82)	(60)	(50)	(40)	42	51
TOTAL-DoE-OTHER ENVIRONMENTAL SERVICES	823	823	403	407	411	(412)	(50)
TOTAL DEPARTMENT OF THE ENVIRONMENT	2,312	2,312	1,737	1,592	1,447	(865)	(37)

TABLE 7.8E DEPARTMENT OF THE ENVIRONMENT (OPENING STATEMENT)

	1986/87 Expend. (Cmnd 9702)	1987/88 Revised Plan	Absolute Change 1987/88- 1986/87	Percent Change 1987/88- 1986/87
	£m	£m	£m	%
Government Grant to Local Government				
Total relevant expenditure	24,251	27,976	3,725	15
Grant (at 45% from 1986/87 outturn)	11,815	12,729	914	8

TABLE 7.8F   DEPARTMENT OF THE ENVIRONMENT (OPENING STATEMENT)

	1986/87 Expenditure (Cmnd 9702)	1986/87 Estimated Outturn	1987/88 Revised Plan	1988/89 Revised Plan	1989/90 Plan	Absolute Change 1989/90-1986/87	Percentage Change 1989/90-1986/87
	£m	£m	£m	£m	£m	£m	%
Government Grant to Local Government							
Total relevant expenditure	24,251	26,400	27,976	29,375	30,844	6,593	27
Grant (at 45% from 1986/87 outturn)	11,815	11,815	12,729	13,366	14,034	2,219	19

7.9 Home Office and Lord Chancellor's Department

Nicholas Deakin

Introduction

1.   As colleagues will be aware, the area loosely defined as 'law and order' experienced one of the largest of all planned increases in expenditure under the last Government.

2.   The manifesto on which we fought the General Election contains a number of radical proposals for changes in policy in this field. However, these do not by any means all imply net increases in public expenditure. Some of the new initiatives can be funded by transfer of resources between programme heads. Others do not require additional resources, but better use of sums already allocated.

3.   Two important examples of areas where funds could be more efficiently deployed are the prison building programme (the largest single capital item in the present budget) and police wages (the main item of current expenditure). It is highly questionable whether tax and ratepayers have received proper value for the very substantial sums spent recently under these two heads.

4.   The total sum bid for by the two Departments (which, by agreement with the Lord Chancellor, are being treated as one unit for the purposes of this exercise), therefore do not greatly exceed the sums projected in Cmnd 9702. For the first year of programmes for which this Government is wholly responsible (1987/88), the proposed increase, when inflation at the projected rate is taken into account, does not substantially exceed the average percentage figure set by the Chancellor.   However, this should not be taken as evidence that no major changes in the direction and emphasis of policy are planned. These will take effect in the later part of the planning period and will have important implications for resource allocation.

5.   In broad terms, our policies have five main elements:

-    a fundamental revision of the criminal justice system, involving basic changes in sentencing policy intended to reduce the number and length of prison sentences passed, together with the decriminalisation of a number of activities;

- a radical overhaul of the penal system, the object of which is to ensure that by the end of our term of office a prison population of less than half the present size is housed in modern accommodation under humane conditions;

- changes in functions and objectives set for the police, designed to secure a change in identity from police *force* to police *service;*

- the introduction of a humane, efficient and non-racial system of immigration control; and

- an unambiguous commitment to the implementation of an effective equal opportunities policy.

6.   All these policies will involve drastic changes in current policies and practices. They are bound to prove controversial, and to involve a substantial amount of parliamentary time. Their introduction will therefore need to be carefully phased in order that we can proceed to implement them fully during the period of our current term of office. The budgets submitted reflect that approach.

7.   Finally, these policy changes will need to be supplemented by structural reforms. The Lord Chancellor and I propose to introduce legislation early in this Session to overhaul the machinery of our two Departments and restructure them into a Ministry of the Justice, responsible for the courts and judiciary and equal opportunities, including a new Office of Civil Liberties, and a Ministry of the Interior, responsible for prisons, police and fire services, and immigration and nationality. (Although these changes will be introduced and implemented as a matter of high priority, the estimates of future expenditure are for convenience presented on the present departmental basis.)

8.   The proposals that follow should be read in the context of these broad commitments.

Justifications for major changes proposed

Court Services (Programme 9.1: projected increase 64%)

These increases reflect a general move towards greater use of the lower courts as part of the broader process of replacing imprisonment wherever possible by other penalties. This involves increases both in court personnel and the building programme, though this will be partly offset by increased revenue from fines. The sums spent on legal aid are also projected to increase, in line with the previous Government's forecast. The functions of the Criminal Injuries Compensation Board and the size of awards that can be made will also be expanded, if legislation is approved. Greater use will be made of conciliation. There will be some offsetting savings through reductions in the responsibilities of higher courts and the introduction of the Crown Prosecution Service. The numbers of the higher judiciary will be reduced; and there will be salary savings *pro rata.*

Penal System (Programme 9.2: projected increase 35%)

Changes here reflect the shift in penal policy referred to above and in particular the reduction in the numbers and duration of sentences of imprisonment passed. Initial expenditure on the prison building programme is in line with the previous Government's forecasts; but the main emphasis will be switched to modernisation and no major new establishments will be constructed once those now in the pipeline have been completed. A programme of closures will be instituted as soon as the fall in the prison population is clearly established; it may be possible to raise funds by sales in the case of a few better preserved local prisons. Taken together with cancellations of new buildings and an eventual fall in the numbers of prison staff employed, this should enable savings to be made towards the end of the planning period. However, these savings will be offset by the commitment to rapid expansion of alternatives to custodial treatment, including reparation and community service, which will be the responsibility of the probation service.

Immigration (Programme 9.5: projected increase 58%)

Additional expenditure here is directed towards securing a more efficient and humane system, in line with manifesto commitments. At present, a large queue of those legally eligible for admission has been allowed to build up. Delay has been employed as a device for keeping down numbers coming in annually; this is a demoralising approach for all concerned and ultimately self-defeating, since all those in the queue will eventually be admitted. The reforms to be introduced will accelerate the process, largely by improving facilities in the countries of origin; they will not affect the absolute totals of admissions. Better training facilities and a systematic programme of recruitment of members of ethnic minority groups account for the rest of the increase.

Fire Service (Programme 9.6: projected increase 19%)

The increase here is partly accounted for by the absorption of the civil emergency element from civil defence (this programme having been abolished) and partly by increased commitments in the first two years as a result of developments in inner city areas.

Community Service (Programme 9.7: projected increase 580%)

Substantial increases are projected here as a result of the policy decision to extend the equal opportunities programme. This will involve a greatly expanded role for the Equal Opportunities Commission (EOC), which will be given substantial additional resources for grants to local authorities and voluntary bodies and concomitant staffing increases. The Voluntary Services Unit (VSU) will also have its functions and resources expanded. The Commission for Racial Equality (CRE) will be the subject of an early independent review. Depending on the outcome, there may also be a further expansion in this area. Finally, the proposed Office of Civil Liberties will be funded at the end of the planning period from this programme.

Conclusion

9.   Almost all the increases referred to above are policy led. It should be noted that there is one programme area (9.3, Police) for which no increase is projected, despite the fact that demographic pressures have been present (the disproportionate propensity of young males, whose numbers have until recently been increasing, to commit crimes). The intention is to deal with pressures in this area by efficiency savings; the case for increased expenditure on modern equipment is not, in our judgement, made out. One programme area (9.4: Civil Defence) is to be wholly eliminated, and residual functions transferred elsewhere. In the area of court services (9.1), some changes occur as a result of increases in public sector costs, within the legal system.

10.   Detailed proposals under all sub-programme heads covering the whole planning period are now set out, as requested, in Tables 7.9A and 7.9B, attached.

TABLE 7.9A   HOME OFFICE AND LORD CHANCELLOR'S DEPARTMENT

	1986/87 Expend. (Cmnd 9702)	1987/88 Revised Plan	Absolute Change 1987/88- 1986/87	Percent Change 1987/88- 1986/87
	£m	£m	£m	%
9.1 COURT SERVICES				
Courts				
Central government	153	90	(63)	(41)
Local authorities				
- Current	169	180	11	7
- Capital	29	40	11	38
Receipts	(161)	(200)	(39)	24
	190	110	(80)	(42)
Criminal Injuries Compensation Board	40	180	140	350
Legal Aid	381	550	169	44
Others	53	50	(3)	(6)
SUB-TOTAL	664	890	226	34
9.2 PENAL SYSTEM				
Prisons	700	700	0	0
Probation and After Care				
Central government	24	60	36	150
Local authorities				
- Current	171	330	159	93
- Capital	6	40	34	567
	201	430	229	114
SUB-TOTAL	901	1,130	229	25
9.3 POLICE				
Central government	88	80	(8)	(9)
Local authorities				
- Current	2,863	2,860	(3)	0
- Capital	92	92	0	0
SUB-TOTAL	3,043	3,032	(11)	0
9.4 CIVIL DEFENCE				
Central government	48	0	(48)	(100)
Local authorities				
- Current	15	0	(15)	(100)
- Capital	2	0	(2)	(100)
SUB-TOTAL	65	0	(65)	(100)
9.5 IMMIGRATION				
Immigration Control	51	90	39	76
Passport Office	25	35	10	40
SUB-TOTAL	76	125	49	64

Contd...

TABLE 7.9A   HOME OFFICE AND LORD CHANCELLOR'S DEPARTMENT (Contd.)

	1986/87 Expend. (Cmnd 9702)	1987/88 Revised Plan	Absolute Change 1987/88- 1986/87	Percent Change 1987/88- 1986/87
	£m	£m	£m	%
9.6 FIRE SERVICE				
Central government	11	40	29	264
Local authorities				
- Current	617	680	63	10
- Capital	21	50	29	138
SUB-TOTAL	649	770	121	19
9.7 COMMUNITY SERVICES				
SUB-TOTAL	25	95	70	280
9.8 MISCELLANEOUS & CENTRAL SERVICES				
SUB-TOTAL	108	108	0	0
TOTAL HOME OFFICE & LORD CHANCELLOR'S DEPARTMENT	5,531	6,150	619	11

Contd......

TABLE 7.9B HOME OFFICE AND LORD CHANCELLOR'S DEPARTMENT

	1986/87 Expend. [Cmnd 9702] £m	1986/87 Estimated Outturn £m	1987/88 Revised Plan £m	1988/89 Revised Plan £m	1989/90 Plan £m	Absolute Change 1989/90-1986/87 £m	Percent Change 1989/90-1986/87 %
9.1 COURT SERVICES							
Courts							
Central government	153	153	90	85	80	(73)	(48)
Local authorities							
– Current	169	169	180	190	200	31	18
– Capital	29	29	40	45	50	21	72
Receipts	(161)	(161)	(200)	(220)	(240)	(79)	49
Criminal Injuries Compensation Board	40	40	180	260	300	260	650
Legal Aid	381	381	550	600	650	269	71
Others	53	53	50	48	46	(7)	(13)
SUB-TOTAL	664	664	890	1,008	1,086	422	64
9.2 PENAL SYSTEM							
Prisons	700	700	700	630	550	(150)	(21)
Probation and After Care							
Government	24	24	60	70	80	56	233
Local Authority							
– Current	171	171	330	430	520	349	204
– Capital	6	6	40	60	70	64	1,067
	201	201	430	560	670	469	233
SUB-TOTAL	901	901	1,130	1,190	1,220	319	35
9.3 POLICE							
Central government	88	88	80	75	70	(18)	(20)
Local authorities							
– Current	2,863	2,863	2,860	2,860	2,860	(3)	(0)
– Capital	92	92	92	85	80	(12)	(13)
SUB-TOTAL	3,043	3,043	3,032	3,020	3,010	(33)	(1)

TABLE 7.9B HOME OFFICE AND LORD CHANCELLOR'S DEPARTMENT (Continued)

	1986/87 Expend. [Cmnd 9702] £m	1986/87 Estimated Outturn £m	1987/88 Revised Plan £m	1988/89 Revised Plan £m	1989/90 Plan £m	Absolute Change 1989/90-1986/87 £m	Percent Change 1989/90-1986/87 %
9.4 CIVIL DEFENCE							
Central government	48	48	0	0	0	(48)	(100)
Local authorities							
— Current	15	15	0	0	0	(15)	(100)
— Capital	2	2	0	0	0	(2)	(100)
SUB-TOTAL	65	65	0	0	0	(65)	(100)
9.5 IMMIGRATION							
Immigration Control	51	51	90	100	85	34	67
Passport Office	25	25	35	37	35	10	40
SUB-TOTAL	76	76	125	137	120	44	58
9.6 FIRE SERVICE							
Central government	11	11	40	40	40	29	264
Local authorities							
— Current	617	617	680	690	670	53	9
— Capital	21	21	50	55	60	39	186
SUB-TOTAL	649	649	770	785	770	121	19
9.7 COMMUNITY SERVICES							
SUB-TOTAL	25	25	95	120	170	145	580
9.8 MISCELLANEOUS & CENTRAL SERVICES							
SUB-TOTAL	108	108	108	105	100	(8)	(7)
TOTAL — HOME OFFICE & LORD CHANCELLOR'S DEPARTMENT	5,531	5,531	6,150	6,365	6,476	945	17

7.10 Department of Education & Science

Due to the illness and then the death of the Education 'minister' participating in the earlier meetings, it has not been possible to include a detailed bid for the DES. Summary Table 7A assumes that DES spending will increase at the same percentage as the bids for which detailed proposals were received.

7.11 Department of Health & Social Security

Michael O'Higgins

1.   The DHSS bid seeks £2,219m more than provided for in Cmnd 9702 in the 1987/88 financial year, rising to an additional £3,159m in 1988/89. The rising bid reflects both the time taken for new projects to come on stream (so that not all the additional funds asked for in the second year could be effectively spent in the first year), and the Department's view that both the social and other policy interests of the Government would be served by other forms of spending increases in the first year.

2.   In particular, we would support the provision of a large share of the additional £5bn in the first year to construction and repair programmes, particularly in the housing area, with this share declining over the following two years as other programmes are able to bring on stream initiatives with longer start-up times.   The employment and economic benefits of a boost to housing spending do not need to be repeated here, and the reduction in unemployment would relieve some of the increasing pressure on this Department's programmes.   In addition, however, we would wish to see housing initiatives specifically targeted on providing housing units for the elderly and on providing for the homeless.   The former would enable more elderly people to release under-occupied housing, increasing their own resources and allowing the housing to be occupied by those more likely to be able to maintain it. The latter would address a pressing social problem, and would also save this Department resources currently being inefficiently and expensively spent on providing bed and breakfast-style board and lodgings for those without proper accommodation.

3.   The total increase requested takes account of the latest projections for the 1986/87 outturn, and includes monies both to correct underestimates on the non-cash limited programmes and for policy developments.   Table 7.11A gives a detailed breakdown for 1987/88 of the uplift as compared to the Cmnd 9702 plans.   The following sections discuss each element of this uplift for 1987/88 and succeeding years.

Hospital and Community Health Services (HCHS)

4.   The additional £632m comprises three elements. First, as indicated in the projected outturn data in Table 7.11B, 1986/87 spending is expected to be £37m above the Cmnd 9702 figure. This is due to the additional funding which was agreed from the Contingency Reserve in order to assist health authorities with the financing of the doctors' and nurses' pay award, and increases the base for 1987/88 spending. The ongoing costs of this award are provided for in the second element of the increase: £325m to provide for a real salary increase to health service employees. Apart from the fact that many of them have experienced a 'negative relative pay effect' in recent years, a trend which cannot be sustained, morale in the service is low, with consequential effects on patient care, and a modest salary boost would be the most immediately effective way to improve both.

5.   The remaining £250m is intended to be the first step towards remedying recent funding inadequacies in the hospital service. In the three years 1983/84 to 1985/86 the volume of resources devoted to HCHS increased by only a total of 0.4% and the 1986/87 rise (which depends on the Whitley Council Settlement) is unlikely to reach 1%. Even allowing for the cash-releasing cost-improvement programme, services in recent years have failed to expand to match demographic and other pressures. (2% annual service growth is necessary to do this.) The DHSS estimate is that, even allowing for the cost-improvement resources, HCHS spending in 1985/86 was some £456m below the level necessary for it to have met the 2% target since 1981/82 (or £686m short if the cash-releasing cost-improvements are ignored).

6.   The further additional funding for 1988/89 consists of £300m to eliminate the shortfall and allow for service improvements, £100m for a slight increase in real wage and salary levels, and £100m as a central pool from which awards will be issued in response to bids which promise to respond to and treat particular DHSS policy concerns. The existence of this pool would be announced the previous year in order to allow health authorities and others time to plan and prepare initiatives, and is experimental. The areas in which bids would be invited are projects which would reduce socioeconomic inequalities in health care access and health status, and projects which would deal with waiting lists in certain specific areas of treatment where demand is finite and effective treatment regimes are available (for example, hip replacements and coronary by-passes). For 1989/90, the cash bid is 5.5% greater than the revised 1988/89 base and so allows 2.5% beyond the projected general rate of inflation for real salary rises (1%) and extra resources (1.5%); the

remaining resources to meet the 2% target will come from the cost-improvement programme.

Family Practitioner Services

7.   The revised plans allow an addition of £110m in 1987/88 and £210m in 1988/89. The former reflects the likelihood that continued rises in the drugs bill mean that the Cmnd 9702 figure is an underestimate (the 1986/87 outturn is projected to be higher for the same reason). This error in recent years has been of the order of £100m. The £210m provides for this correction and also for the implementation of the decisions which will result from the current consultations on the Primary Health Care Green Paper. Whatever the decisions are, some lubrication of their implementation will be required. The extra capital spending in 1987/88 reflects the higher outturn expected this year; thereafter it provides for any additional capital needed in consequence of Primary Health Care.

8.   The additional resources for central health and miscellaneous services - £20m in 1987/88 - are to provide for services connected with AIDS.

Personal Social Services

9.   As these are a local authority responsibility, the bid follows convention and simply projects forward this year's likely outturn. It should be noted that this is, as usual, more than projected in the White Paper. Next year's outturn will, we expect, be some £200m greater than this revised projection, a sum which will have to be found from the Contingency Reserve.

Social Security

10.   Social security spending outturn in recent years has consistently run above plan by more than £1bn, partly because of higher unemployment and partly because average costs per claimant have been greater than anticipated (due to greater numbers of dependants etc.) These factors continue to be present, though their impact should not be quite so great. In addition, however, the Cmnd 9702 plans

underestimate spending because of:

(a)   the continued rise in supplementary benefit spending for private and voluntary residential care of the elderly;

(b)   the decision to extend eligibility for the invalid care allowance to married women; and

(c)   the failure to carry successfully into legislation the various savings projected for future years in the social security reform plans (such as reducing the DHSS liability to pay the rates of claimants). These affect the plans for 1988/89 and 1989/90.

11.   The revised plans assume that outturn in 1986/87 will be £818m greater than assumed in Cmnd 9702 because of estimating errors, and that the plans for subsequent years need to be increased by £1,100m to take account of these factors. The revised plans allow a further £640m in 1987/88 and £900m in 1988/89 for policy developments.

12.   We have four major policy priorities in social security: the elderly, the long-term unemployed, families and the care of the infirm and disabled.

13.   While there is pressure for a real increase in the basic pension, we do not wish to use resources so unselectively. Newer cohorts of elderly people increasingly have significant other resources, notably from occupational pension and from the maturing of SERPS. To increase the basic pension would be to add further to those resources. This affluence among the elderly is, however, partial; those - increasingly the older elderly - without SERPS or private resources are in need of assistance. Whilst a £4 weekly increase in the basic pension would cost over £2bn, a similar increase in the supplementary pension would cost around £450m (£380m to existing recipients, and £70m to those who would become eligible because of the increased level). This is provided for from 1987/88 onwards.

14.   Two further advantages of this increase should be noted. First, it will provide an immediate boost to demand, primarily for British-produced goods, so assisting with the Government's plans to reduce unemployment. Second, it is an increase which will diminish over time, as fewer of the elderly will lack additional pensions and other resources.

15.   The remaining £190m in 1987/88 will go to assistance to the long-term unemployed (£70m) and to Family Income Supplement (FIS)

(£120m). There is strong evidence that the former are particularly badly off, while the proportion of children living in families in poverty has risen sharply in recent years. To avoid labour market disincentives among those potentially re-employable, the £70m will be concentrated on the older unemployed (whose chances of ever working again are slight) by extending down from 60 the age at which the long-term unemployed may receive the higher rate of supplementary benefit (and come off the unemployment register).

16.   In 1988/89, FIS is to be transformed into a Family Credit, which will be operated on a net income assessment to diminish the poverty trap problem. With this obstacle to selective assistance to working families reduced, a further £120m will be allocated (representing a boost of £240m over current plans). Within a couple of years it should be technically feasible to operate a tax credit system, so that much of this spending, and that on child benefit, can be transformed into tax spending.

17.   The remaining £140m in the 1988/89 bid, and the further additional resources for 1989/90, are in respect of the care of the infirm and disabled. The results of the current Disability Needs Survey will be available to guide us - and will require extra resources - by then, and there is in any case a clear necessity for a coherent policy in respect of this care. At present, it may be financed through benefits such as attendance allowance and invalid care allowance; through the supplementary benefit system paying for private residential care; or through local authority or NHS provision for care in the community. In consultation with local authorities etc., we wish to develop an integrated strategy whereby the total resources available for care in this area may be used in the manner most appropriate to each individual needing care, rather than, as at present, the form of assistance depending upon the programme from which assistance is available. In designing the new system, a guiding principle will be that the resources should be both adequate for and available to families or individuals who would prefer to care themselves for disabled or infirm dependants. It is intended that the new policy should come into operation in January 1989; hence the £140m represents the part-year cost of the initiative.

18.   The increased resources represent only a small rise in the size of the social security budget, but, used in this way, will achieve a lot. In particular, the combination of the real rise in supplementary pensions and the development and resourcing of the new policy on caring (a policy benefiting carers as well as those cared for) can be represented as a major government initiative to address the problems of, and to help, the growing numbers of over 75s in the country.

TABLE 7.11A DEPARTMENT OF HEALTH AND SOCIAL SECURITY

	1986/87 Expend. (Cmnd 9702)	1987/88 Revised Plan	Absolute Change 1987/88-1986/87	Percent Change 1987/88-1986/87
	£m	£m	£m	%
HEALTH SERVICES				
11.1 Hospital & Community Health Services				
Current spending				
- gross	10,366	11,472	1,106	11
- charges	(86)	(90)	(4)	5
- net	10,280	11,382	1,102	11
Capital spending	765	790	25	3
11.1 Family Practitioner Services				
Current spending				
- gross	3,899	4,250	351	9
- charges	(382)	(410)	(28)	7
- net	3,517	3,840	323	9
Capital spending	11	13	2	18
11.3 Central Health & Miscellaneous Services				
Current spending				
- gross	500	540	40	8
- charges	(9)	(10)	(1)	11
- net	491	530	39	8
Capital spending	17	20	3	18
NATIONAL HEALTH SERVICE Totals				
Current spending				
- gross	14,765	16,262	1,497	10
- net	14,288	15,752	1,464	10
Capital spending	793	823	30	4
PERSONAL SOCIAL SERVICES				
Current spending				
- gross	2,954	3,130	176	6
- charges	(419)	(420)	(1)	0
- net	2,535	2,710	175	7
Capital spending	79	79	0	0
General Practice Finance Corporation	27	30	3	11
HEALTH & PERSONAL SOCIAL SERVICES Totals				
Current spending				
- gross	17,719	19,392	1,673	9
- charges	(896)	(930)	(34)	4
- net	16,823	18,462	1,639	10
Capital spending	899	932	33	4
TOTAL DHSS - HPSS NET	17,722	19,394	1,672	9
TOTAL DHSS - SOCIAL SECURITY	42,932	46,140	3,208	7
TOTAL DHSS	60,654	65,534	4,880	8

144

TABLE 7.11B DEPARTMENT OF HEALTH AND SOCIAL SECURITY

	1986/87 Expenditure (Cmnd 9702) £m	1986/87 Estimated Outturn £m	1987/88 Revised Plan £m	1988/89 Revised Plan £m	1989/90 Plan £m	Absolute Change 1989/90-1986/87 £m	Percentage Change 1989/90-1986/87 %
HEALTH SERVICES							
11.1 Hospital & Community Health Services							
Current spending – gross	10,366	10,423	11,472	12,480	13,170	2,804	27
– charges	(86)	(86)	(90)	(100)	(100)	(14)	16
– net	10,280	10,337	11,382	12,380	13,070	2,790	27
Capital spending	765	768	790	810	820	55	7
11.1 Family Practitioner services							
Current spending – gross	3,899	4,000	4,250	4,580	4,860	961	25
– charges	(382)	(390)	(410)	(430)	(450)	(68)	18
– net	3,517	3,610	3,840	4,150	4,410	893	25
Capital spending	11	14	13	15	18	7	64
11.3 Central Health & Miscellaneous Services							
Current spending – gross	500	518	540	580	610	110	22
– charges	(9)	(9)	(10)	(10)	(10)	(1)	11
– net	491	509	530	570	600	109	22
Capital spending	17	20	20	20	22	5	29
NATIONAL HEALTH SERVICE Totals							
Current spending – gross	14,765	14,941	16,262	17,640	18,640	3,875	26
– net	14,288	14,456	15,752	17,100	18,080	3,792	27
Capital spending	793	802	823	845	860	67	8
PERSONAL SOCIAL SERVICES							
Current spending – gross	2,954	3,130	3,130	3,130	3,130	176	6
– charges	(419)	(420)	(420)	(420)	(420)	(1)	0
– net	2,535	2,710	2,710	2,710	2,710	175	7
Capital spending	79	79	79	79	79	0	0
General Practice Finance Corporation	27	30	30	32	35	8	30
HEALTH & PERS. SOCIAL SERVICES Totals							
Current spending – gross	17,719	18,071	19,392	20,770	21,770	4,051	23
– charges	(896)	(905)	(930)	(960)	(980)	(84)	9
– net	16,823	17,166	18,462	19,810	20,790	3,967	24
Capital spending	899	911	932	956	974	75	8
TOTAL DHSS – HPSS NET	17,722	18,077	19,394	20,766	21,764	4,042	23
TOTAL DHSS – SOCIAL SECURITY	42,932	43,750	46,140	47,900	50,200	7,268	17
TOTAL DHSS	60,654	61,827	65,534	68,666	71,964	11,310	19

7.12 Scotland

James Ross

The Scottish context

1.   Two factors necessitate a unique approach to the construction of a programme for Scotland: the strong Scottish expectation of an Assembly coupled with the uncertainty as to what we are to do about it; and, so long as no Assembly exists, the inevitable interdependence of policy north and south of the border on a number of issues on which there may be a change of direction.

2.   These latter issues include not only those defined as interdependent in Cmnd 9702 but also, notably, education and health and the personal social services.   Any or all of the other services nominally entirely within my control could also be affected if the revised UK programme strongly featured new strategies in these fields.

3.   The question mark hanging over the Assembly has a secondary effect. Our immediate programme decisions will be scrutinised for any signs of our intentions for an Assembly, of the freedom we are likely to give it and of the generosity of the financial base on which it will start off. Conversely, any exceptional generosity shown now is likely to have to be continued if and when the Assembly is established.

Short term strategy

4.   In these circumstances, I propose a two-pronged strategy pending a decision, and if appropriate, a timetable for the Assembly:

(a)   a group of related, but not over-expensive initiatives assured of both relevance and popularity; and

(b)   a close adherence to Cmnd 9702 on other services, particularly those likely to be affected by UK policy.

The close adherence to Cmnd 9702 takes account of the need to allow for inflation where appropriate. Any likely factors which it does not take into account are indicated in the remarks on the services concerned below.

The initiatives

5.   The initiatives are directed towards industrial investment, employment and preservation of fixed assets, relief of urban stress and experiments in community care. The last two have the supplementary, but important, objective of winning favour with the voluntary sector, an articulate and opinion-influencing group with a strong Scottish awareness.

6.   The specific initiatives are:

-     an increase in the amount and range of the industrial investment activities of the Scottish Development Agency (SDA) and the Highlands and Islands Development Board (HIDB);

-     an increase in the maintenance programme on roads;

-     an increase in the housing improvement programme, particularly directed at such problems as damp and structural defect;

-     a substantial increase in the urban programme; and

-     an increase in the support of voluntary agencies developing community care schemes.

Commentary on specific services

Industry, Energy, Trade, Employment and Tourism

7.   The elements of this within my control are the investment and investment promotion activities of the SDA and HIDB. The previous Government restricted both the range and scale of these activities. I propose widening the guidelines of the two organisations to much nearer their original form and making a significant increase in their financial allocations as against Cmnd 9702.

8.   Over the three years of the current projections I propose a cash increase of £2m, £3m and £5m respectively for the HIBD and £5m, £10m and £30m for SDA. In percentage terms, this represents 7-18% over three years for the HIBD and 7-30% for the SDA. These amounts take account of the practicable rate of expansion for both organisations. They should also be considered in light of the sharp drop in the total for this programme between 1986/87 and 1987/88 provided for in Cmnd 9702.

9.   In the same vein, I have thought it undesirable to abide by the appreciable drop in expenditure on tourism envisaged by Cmnd 9702. The revised provision for this does little more, over three years, than allow for inflation. It more realistically reflects the present state of Scottish tourist organisation and facilities.

Roads and Transport

10.   Road maintenance has suffered severely from the attempts at economy under the previous Government. This economy is already threatening to become a diseconomy. Maintenance work creates substantial employment and can be quickly and efficiently put in hand. I propose a cash increase of £30m over Cmnd 9702 in 1987/88. There would be a further cash increase of about half that amount in 1988/89, in addition to provision for inflation.

Housing

11.   Much of the Scottish housing stock, especially the still very substantial local authority housing stock, is in a serious condition. We are already in a situation in which money not spent now will mean far greater expenditure sometime. The scale of the problem is disputable but certainly too great for significant progress to be possible within a few years. However, we can simultaneously increase the rate of attack, provide employment quickly and for some time to come, and bring about a desperately needed improvement in central/local government relations in Scotland.

12.   I propose cash increases over Cmnd 9702 of £20m in 1987/88 and £50m in 1988/89 with a correspondingly increased figure in 1989/90.

13.   Provision under this subhead has been decreasing in real terms for some years but was envisaged as flattening out in 1987/88. Inflation has therefore been taken into account from that year. In addition, I propose as one of my immediate initiatives a substantial increase in the urban programme.

14.   In Scotland, that programme was first encouraged, then severely cut back by the previous Government. So there are a great many schemes in the pipeline which could be approved and put into operation relatively quickly. Mostly, such schemes have to be funded for four years or more. An increase in new commitments in 1987/88, therefore, implies at least as great an increase for the remainder of the forecast period.

15.   I propose a cash increase of £5m for urban aid in 1987/88, rising to £10m in each of the succeeding years.

Education

16.   At the present stage, this programme can be little more than speculation. Teachers' pay and the restructuring of the syllabus are both in the melting pot, the former awaiting the report of the Main Committee. Things are not made easier by the fact that the two are interconnected. (Stop Press: The Main Committee has recommended a salary increase of 16.9% (£250m), in the next two years, which is not explicitly included here.)

17.   The figures in Cmnd 9702 imply a continuing significant decline in real terms through 1988/89. I do not consider that a practicable political stance. I have therefore assumed for the ensuing three years amounts which rather more than cancel the effects of inflation, the increase being weighted towards the end of the period. Making every allowance for falling school rolls, I cannot believe we will need less. The likelihood is that these provisions will not be enough.

Arts and Libraries

18.   This programme also includes leisure and recreation facilities.

Cmnd 9702 presupposes a reduction both in cash and real terms in local authority current, and to a lesser extent, capital expenditure. In the circumstances facing us I regard this as doubtfully realistic and certainly undesirable. My proposed allocations would approximately maintain the 1986/87 provision in real terms.

Health and Personal Social Services

19.   Although pressure to increase this programme will be severe, and although we must create a greater sense of security about the future of the Health Service, I consider that this must be done by better methods and a more resolute selection of strategic priorities. For the Health Service, therefore, I have adhered to the Cmnd 9702 provisions, subject to the qualification below.

20.   I have also adhered to them in the field of social welfare. However, in the context of joint action between the health and social welfare services, I have assumed an extra £10m in 1987/88 specifically for the development of community care schemes, with an emphasis on the contribution that can be made by the voluntary sector. I have assumed double that amount for the same purpose in 1988/89 and about the same in the following year.

The Standstill Services

21.   In relation to all the services in the Scottish list not itemised above, I propose retaining the assumptions and figures of Cmnd 9702, subject to allowance for the prescribed rates of inflation. In these cases I have continued to assume any reduction in real terms underlying Cmnd 9702, except in the case of Law, Order and Protective Services, where Cmnd 9702 assumed from 1988/89 on a reduction in real terms which I do not consider realistic.

Cross-border interaction

22.   I reiterate the point made earlier that the above proposals have been made without full knowledge of the intentions of my colleagues for comparable services in England and Wales, the effects of which cannot necessarily be ignored in Scotland.

TABLE 7.12A   SCOTLAND

	1986/87 Expend. (Cmnd 9702)	1987/88 Revised Plan	Absolute Change 1987/88- 1986/87	Percent Change 1987/88- 1986/87
	£m	£m	£m	%
Agriculture, fisheries, food	190	190	0	0
Industry, energy, trade and employment	302	237	(65)	(22)
Tourism	13	12	(1)	(8)
Roads and transport	587	630	43	7
Housing	645	690	45	7
Other environmental services	588	625	37	6
Law, order and protective services	570	580	10	2
Education	1,792	1,850	58	3
Arts and libraries	75	77	2	3
Health and personal social services	2,443	2,540	97	4
Other public services	110	110	0	0
Local authorities' unallocated current expenditure	19	20	1	5
Nationalised industries' EFLs	239	0	(239)	(100)
TOTAL - SCOTLAND	7,573	7,561	(12)	(0)

151

TABLE 7.12B   SCOTLAND

	1986/87 Expenditure (Cmnd 9702) £m	1986/87 Estimated Outturn £m	1987/88 Revised Plan £m	1988/89 Revised Plan £m	1989/90 Plan £m	Absolute Change 1989/90-1986/87 £m	Percentage Change 1989/90-1986/87 %
Agriculture, fisheries, food	190	190	190	197	203	13	7
Industry, energy, trade and employment	302	302	237	253	280	(22)	(7)
Tourism	13	13	12	14	15	2	15
Roads and transport	587	587	630	650	700	113	19
Housing	645	645	690	750	800	155	24
Other environmental services	588	588	625	660	680	92	16
Law, order and protective services	570	563	580	600	620	50	9
Education	1,792	1,792	1,850	1,950	2,100	308	17
Arts and libraries	75	75	77	80	83	8	11
Health and personal social services	2,443	2,443	2,540	2,650	2,740	297	12
Other public services	110	110	110	114	118	8	7
Local authorities' unallocated current expenditure	19	19	20	20	20	1	5
Nationalised industries' EFLs	239	239		(120)		(239)	(100)
TOTAL SCOTLAND	7,573	7,566	7,561	7,818	8,359	786	10

Citations

British Library (1986) *Current Research in Britain 1986,* London, British Library

Defence Committee (1986) *Statement on the Defence Estimates: Second Report of 1985-86,* HC 399 of Session 1985-86, London, HMSO

Mack, R.P. (1971) *Planning on Uncertainty: Decision Making in Business and Government Administration,* New York, Wiley Inter-Science

Ministry of Defence (1986) *Statement on the Defence Estimates,* Cmnd 9763, London HMSO

Mosley, P. (1985) 'When is a policy instrument not an instrument?: fiscal marksmanship in Britain, 1951-84', *Journal of Public Policy,* Vol.5, pp. 69-86

Public Finance Foundation (1985) *Collective Decision Making in Government,* London, Public Finance Foundation

Public Finance Foundation (1986) *Collective Decision-Making on Public Expenditure,* London, Public Finance Foundation

Rose, R. (1987) *Ministers and Ministries,* Oxford, Clarendon Press

Tarschys, D. (1985) 'Curbing public expenditure: current trends', *Journal of Public Policy,* Vol. 5, pp. 23-68

Treasury (1986a) *The Government's Expenditure Plans 1986-87 to 1988-89,* Cmnd 9702-I,II, London, HMSO

Treasury (1986b) *Financial Statement and Budget Report 1986-87,* HC 273 of Session 1985-86, London, HMSO

Treasury (1986c) *Autumn Statement 1986,* Cm 14, London, HMSO

Treasury (1986d) *The Management of Public Spending,* London, HM Treasury

Treasury (1987) *The Government's Expenditure Plans 1987-88 to 1989-90,* Cm 56-I,II, London, HMSO